MORE PATHWAYS OUT OF POVERTY

MORE PATHWAYS OUT OF POVERTY

Edited by Sam Daley-Harris and Anna Awimbo

Kumarian
Press, Inc.

More Pathways Out of Poverty

Published 2006 in the United States of America by Kumarian Press, Inc., 1294 Blue Hills Avenue, Bloomfield, CT 06002 USA

Design, production, and editorial services were provided by Publication Services, Inc., Champaign, Illinois. The text of this book is set in Adobe Sabon 10.5/13.5

Printed in Canada on acid-free paper by Transcontinental Gagne.
Text printed with vegetable oil-based ink.

∞" The paper used in this publication meets the minimum requirements of the American National Standard for Information Sciences—Permanence of Paper for printed Library Materials, ANSI Z39.48-1984

Library of Congress Cataloging-in-Publication Data

More pathways out of poverty / edited by Sam Daley-Harris and Anna Awimbo.
    p. cm.
    Includes bibliographical references.
    ISBN-13: 978-1-56549-229-5 (pbk. : alk. paper)
    ISBN-10: 1-56549-229-3 (pbk. : alk. paper)
1. Microfinance—Developing countries.   2. Financial institutions—Developing countries.   3. Poverty—Developing countries.   I. Daley-Harris, Sam, 1946–   II. Awimbo, Anna, 1965–
    HG178.33.D44M67 2006
    332.109172'4—dc21   2006023643

11   10   09   08   07   06   05   10   9   8   7   6   5   4   3   2

Contents

Figures and Tables

Figures

Tables

Acknowledgments

This book stands on the shoulders of the first volume of *Pathways Out of Poverty,* which was commissioned and published for the Microcredit Summit + 5 held in 2002 in New York City. Four years have now passed and the Microcredit Summit is set to launch Phase II of the Campaign at the Global Microcredit Summit 2006 in Halifax, Canada. Phase II is focused on two new goals for 2015: (1) reaching 175 million of the world's poorest families with microcredit and (2) ensuring that 100 million of the world's poorest families rise above the US$1/day threshold.

Just as microcredit's very existence depended on breaking some of the basic rules of banking, achieving the Summit's new goals will require shattering standard practice in international development. While we may wish it weren't so, international development continues to fail the very poor, those living on less than US$1 a day. It is their children who are the 100 million children of primary school age not enrolled in school and who die from largely preventable malnutrition and disease at the rate of some 29,000 a day. It is these families the Campaign seeks to empower. The chapters in this book are critical to answering the question of how it can be done.

The ideas for these chapters were developed over a two-year period with input from members of the Campaign through evaluation forms completed at global and regional meetings. The ideas were further developed through feedback from a series of electronic questionnaires. The final input and approval came from the Campaign Executive Committee. Our primary appreciation, however, must go to the authors, who gave so fully of themselves to this endeavor.

In the first chapter, "Achieving the Microcredit Summit and Millennium Development Goals of Reducing Extreme Poverty: What Is the Cutting Edge on Cost-Effectively Measuring Movement across the US$1/Day Threshold?" Thierry van Bastelaer and Manfred Zeller provide groundbreaking information critical to measuring progress toward achievement of these two poverty goals. It is difficult to understand how practitioners around the world in all fields of development continue, six years after the adoption of the Millenium Development Goals, to operate without an inexpensive way of knowing whether progress is being made in helping families rise above the US$1/day threshold. This chapter and the work being done in connection with it will begin to bring about this much-needed change.

The work described in this chapter was supported by the Microenterprise Development Office of the U.S. Agency for International Development through the Accelerated Microenterprise Advancement Project and its Enabling Environment Component. The authors express their gratitude to the researchers involved in this project, in particular Gabriela Alcaraz, Omar Azfar, Brian Beard, Tresja Denysenko, Kate Druschel, Jean-Luc Dubois, Megan Gash, Christiaan Grootaert, Julia Johannsen, Anthony Leegwater, Ann Mestrovich, and Jonathan Morduch, as well as the Advisory Panel for the project.

In the second chapter, "Factors That Contribute to Exponential Growth: Case Studies for Massive Outreach to the Poor and Poorest," Alex Counts, Erin Connor, and Roshaneh Zafar outline the key components of exponential growth, which is critical to reaching the Microcredit Summit's new outreach goal.

The authors wish to thank the following people: Muhammad Yunus, Grameen Bank; John Hatch, FINCA; Chris Dunford, Freedom from Hunger; Larry Reed, Opportunity International; Kate McKee, USAID; Marshall Saunders, Grameen de la Frontera; Phil Smith, Richard Rosenberg and Xavier Reille, CGAP; David Gibbons, CASHPOR-India; Deb Burand, Grameen Foundation; Janet Thompson and Bob Eichfeld, Grameen Foundation Board members; Lawrence Yanovitch, the Bill and Melinda Gates Foundation; Prof. Latifee, Grameen Trust; Dan Norell, World Vision; Dolores Torres, CARD; Godwin Ehigiamusoe, LAPO; Arjun Muralidharan, ASA; Ken Liffiton and Gloria Garrett, Foundation for Women; Ascanio Graziosi and Mosharraf Hossain Khan, PKSF; Shafiqul Mohammed Manik, PUSS; Lamin Manneh, People in Action; Sita Conklin and Mark Edington, Save the Children; Jamal Dadi, USAID; Khawar Ansari, Chairman of Kashf; Kamal Hyat, Pakistan Poverty Alleviation Fund; Steve Jones, DFID; Steve Rasmussen, World Bank; Dr. Wolday Amha, AEMFI; Ayachew Kebede, SIDA; Haile Gyohannes, BOFED; Yared Fekade, GTZ; Aziz Benmaazouz and Leila Akhmisse, Zakoura; and Mekonnen Yelewem wessen and Getaneh Gobezie, ACSI.

In the third chapter "Commercialization: Overcoming the Obstacles to Accessing Commercial Funds While Maintaining a Commitment to Reaching the Poorest," Larry Reed shows the importance of both accessing new sources of funds and remaining true to the institution's social mission. Reed acknowledges the pioneers of microcredit, on whose shoulders we all stand. He also offers his thanks to Julie Felix and Tim Head for assisting in the research; Biju C. Matthew for conducting interviews in India; the sixteen interviewees for giving so generously of their time and wisdom; Adrian Gonzalez for providing statistical analysis of the MIX data for the author; Richard Rosenberg, Syed Hashemi, Elizabeth Littlefield, Susy Cheston, and

Kristi Yuthas for carefully reviewing the text and providing suggestions that greatly improved the final product; and the clients of microfinance, whose hard work, entrepreneurial skills and integrity make this work possible.

In the final chapter, "Building Domestic Financial Systems That Work for the Majority," Women's World Banking provides insight into another key area that can either contribute to or impede progress toward using microfinance to reduce poverty. Forty representatives contributed their ideas and feedback to the original document on which this chapter is based, and Women's World Banking wishes to thank them for their initial contribution. Nancy Barry and Nicola Armacost made significant contributions to the effort.

This book is vital to forwarding the Campaign's learning agenda and its view that the very poor can find a dignified route out of poverty if only they are given the opportunity. We are indebted to the authors for their contribution to this work. The opinions expressed, however, are those of the authors and do not necessarily reflect the views of the Campaign or of any other organization.

Anna Awimbo, the Campaign's Research Director and my co-editor, has played the greatest role in shepherding this book to completion. She has worked tirelessly with the authors, case study subjects, and others to bring this work to fruition, and for this I am in her debt. As with all of the Campaign's work, I remain in awe of the contribution to this audacious project made by my staff: Nelson Agyemang, Armando Boquin, Bill Campbell, Trenton DuVal, Michelle Gomperts, Lisa Marie Laegreid, Brian McConnell, Felicia Montgomery, Kathy Morrell, Dalia Palchik, Dr. D.S.K. Rao, Barnabé Schwartz, and Sean Whalen.

Krishna Sondhi, Jim Lance, and their team at Kumarian Press contribute each day to building a better world through the books they publish and the work they champion. It is an honor to work with them.

We have also been privileged to have worked with Susan Yates and the team at Publication Services.

Special thanks go to the following donors who funded some portion of the material in this book: Austrian Development Agency, Citigroup Foundation, the International Fund for Agricultural Development, and the Open Society Institute.

There are so many others who have offered their feedback or contributed in some other way to this book. To those we have not mentioned, we extend our apologies and our deepest gratitude.

Preface

The world stands at a crossroads. One path leads to the end of poverty by 2025. On this path, extreme poverty is cut in half and the other Millennium Development Goals (MDGs) are achieved by 2015, goals agreed to six years ago by more than 180 heads of state and government at the United Nations Millennium Summit.

But if we are not vigilant and committed, we could easily follow a second path, and see only limited change to the harrowing realities faced by far too many people on this planet: one billion people living on less than US$1 a day; 100 million children of primary school age not in school; and 29,000 children under the age of five dying *each day* from largely *preventable* malnutrition and disease. Which course will we take?

The Microcredit Summit Campaign leads the way toward the first path, the road leading to the end of poverty. Our compass is the Campaign's new set of goals for 2015: (1) reaching 175 million of the world's poorest families with microcredit, affecting 875 million family members, and (2) ensuring that 100 million of the world's poorest families rise above the US$1/day threshold, lifting 500 million family members out of extreme poverty.

This book and its predecessor are roadmaps for reaching the end of poverty. Written for the Global Microcredit Summit held November 12–15, 2006, in Halifax, Canada, it outlines critical issues and warns against diversions that can distract us from our ultimate goal: an end to the scandal of global poverty.

In the first chapter, "Achieving the Microcredit Summit and Millennium Development Goals of Reducing Extreme Poverty: What Is the Cutting Edge on Cost-Effectively Measuring Movement across the $1/Day Threshold?" Thierry van Bastelaer of the University of Maryland and Manfred Zeller of the University of Hohenheim argue that tools developed to cost-effectively measure US$1/day poverty could also measure movement across the US$1/day line, if certain conditions are met.

In the following chapter, "Factors That Contribute to Exponential Growth: Case Studies for Massive Outreach to the Poor and Poorest," Alex Counts and Erin Connor of Grameen Foundation and Roshaneh Zafar of Kashf Foundation outline the key ingredients to exponential growth so that

MFI leaders, boards, funders, investors, and governments will be better able to fuel this movement toward the end of poverty.

Next, "Commercialization: Overcoming the Obstacles to Accessing Commercial Funds While Maintaining a Commitment to Reaching the Poorest," by Larry Reed of Opportunity International, shows that while the move toward commercialization can bring greater access to commercial financing and allow institutions to collect voluntary savings, it can also pull institutions away from their social mission and away from poorer clients. Reed argues that this doesn't have to be the case.

In the chapter "Building Domestic Financial Systems That Work for the Majority," Women's World Banking guides policymakers and practitioners in thinking about how to build country strategies in the areas of (1) policy; (2) creating institutional structures such as autonomous microfinance funds, rating agencies, and credit bureaus; (3) retail capacity; and (4) a range of products from loans and savings to remittance and insurance products.

The microfinance movement was created by development revolutionaries, people who broke the rules of banking and overcame the failures of international development. They offered tiny, uncollateralized loans to poor, illiterate women and successfully reached and empowered the very poor through self-sustaining institutions, something international development still struggles to do.

Now the field is increasingly moving into the world of commercial finance, as it should, and is being increasingly adopted by international aid agencies, which is entirely appropriate. But neither sector is able to ensure that the progress made to date translates into a dramatic reduction in global poverty. That is where the Microcredit Summit Campaign and documents like this come in.

Successful social movements bring a compelling vision and a commitment to overcoming barriers. This is true whether the goal is to secure the vote for women in the United States or to end apartheid in South Africa. The Microcredit Summit Campaign and its goals are no different, especially the goal of ensuring that 100 million of the world's poorest families rise above the US$1/day threshold. The Campaign is a kind of "civil rights" movement for the hundreds of millions of families living on less than $1/day. We know that they can leave poverty with dignity, provided the barriers discussed in this book are overcome.

We stand with women like Sufia Begum, a former beggar from Mothbaria in the district of Feni in Bangladesh. Sufia married Bachhu Mia before she was thirteen years old. They had three children, but her husband married again and abandoned her and the children, whom Sufia had great difficulty feeding. Many times they were forced to starve along with her. The children didn't attend school, and the family slept on the ground.

With no other way to survive, Sufia Begum resorted to begging. "There's nothing in my stomach," she would tell passersby. "For God's sake, would you please give me some food?"

One day Sufia met Monwara, president of Basanti Landless Women's Group, members of ASA Bangladesh. Monwara told Sufia about the loan program for the hard-core poor. Sufia worried that she would not be able to repay a loan, but Monwara encouraged her and Sufia took a loan of about $40, which she used to purchase dried fish, biscuits, nuts, chocolate, and other foods.

From her town in the Feni district, Sufia traveled to small, rural villages to sell her goods. Instead of begging, Sufia began asking, "Do you need churi, shanka, dried fish, or chocolate?" Gradually, the villagers came to see her as a regular trader and became routine customers. Sufia carried the food in a basket that rested atop her head.

Sufia repaid her loan and took another loan of about $80, so that she could expand her business. With the profits she has generated, Sufia bought a cot for her children to sleep on and put a tin roof on her family's house.

It is to women like Sufia Begum and her hundreds of million sisters around the world that this book is dedicated. For it is they who are the inspiration, as they build their pathways out of poverty.

Sam Daley-Harris
June 14, 2006

Acronyms

ACCION	Americans for Community Co-operation in Other Nations, International
ACLEDA	Association of Cambodian Local Economic Development Agencies
ACSI	Amhara Credit and Savings Institution
ADOPEM	*Asociación Dominicana para el Desarrollo de la Mujer*
AEMFI	Association for Ethiopian Microfinance Institutions
AFMIN	The Africa Microfinance Network
AGAPE	Asociación General para Asesorar Pequeñas Empresas (Colombia)
AIMS	Assessing the Impact of Microfinance Services
AKF	Aga Khan Foundation
AMFIU	Association of Microenterprise Finance Institutions of Uganda
ASA	Association for Social Advancement (Bangladesh)
ATM	Automated teller machine
BANCOLDEX	Banco de Comercio Exterior de Colombia
BOFED	Bureau of Finance and Economic Deveolopment (Ethiopia)
BPAC	Balanced Poverty Accuracy Criterion
BRAC	Bangladesh Rural Advancement Committee
BRI	Bank Rakyat Indonesia
CARD	Centre for Agriculture and Rural Development
CASHPOR	Network for Credit and Savings for the Hard-Core Poor
CBE	Central Bank of Ethiopia
CEO	Chief Executive Officer
CFC	Commercial finance corporation
CFTS	CASHPOR Financial & Technical Services Limited
CGAP	Consultative Group to Assist the Poor
CIDA	Canadian International Development Agency
COOPI	Cooperazione Internazionale
CRECER	Credito con Educacion Rural (Bolivia)
DESA	Department of Economic and Social Affairs (UN)

DFID	Department for International Development
ENIGH	Encuesta Nacional de Ingresos y Gastos de los Hogares
FADES	Fundación para Alternativas de Desarrollo (Bolivia)
FELABAN	Federación Latinoamericana de Bancos
FFH	Freedom from Hunger
FINCA	Foundation for International Community Assistance
FWWB	Friends of Women's World Banking
GF	Grameen Foundation
GNBI	Global Network for Banking Innovation
GNI	Gross national income
GTZ	Geseuschafür Techish Zusammenarbeit (Germany)
HIID/BRI	Harvard Institute for International Development/Bank Rakyat Indonesia
HIV/AIDS	Human immunodeficiency virus/acquired immunodeficiency syndrome
HIVOS	Humanistisch Instituut voor Ontwikkelingssamenwerking (The Netherlands)
ICDDR,B	International Centre for Diarrhoeal Disease Research (Bangladesh)
ICT	Information communication technology
IDB	Inter-American Development Bank
IFAD	International Fund for Agricultural Development
IT	Information technology
KMBI	Kabalikat para sa Maunlad na Buhay, Inc. (Philippines)
LAPO	Lift Above Poverty Organization (Nigeria)
LSMS	Living Standards Measurement Survey
MAD	Moroccan dirham(s)
MBB	Microbanking Bulletin
MCRIL	Micro Credit Ratings International Limited
MCS	Microcredit Summit Campaign
MDI	Microfinance Deposit-Taking Institution
MDG	Millennium Development Goals
MFI	Microfinance institution
MIS	Management information system
MIX	Microfinance Information Exchange
NABARD	National Bank for Agriculture and Rural Development (India)
NBFC	Nonbank financial corporation
NDB	National Development Bank

NGO	Nongovernmental organization
OER	Operating expense ratio
OIBM	Opportunity International Bank of Malawi
OISASL	Opportunity International Sinapi Aba Savings and Loans Company Limited (Ghana)
ORDA	Organization for the Rehabilitation and Development of Amhara
PADME	Association Pour La Promotion Et L'Appui Au Developpment De Micro-Enterprises
PAR	Portfolio at risk
PAT	Poverty Assessment Tool
PIE	Poverty Incidence Error
PKSF	Palli Karma Sahayak Foundation (Bangladesh)
PMN	Pakistan Microfinance Network
PPAF	Pakistan Poverty Alleviation Fund
PPI	Progress out of Poverty Index
PPP	Purchasing power parity
RUFIP	Rural Financial Intermediation Programme
SACCO	Saving and Credit Cooperative
SC	Save the Children
SDA-IS	Social Dimensions of Adjustment Integrated Survey
SEEP	Small Enterprise and Education Promotion Network
SEF	Small Enterprise Foundation (South Africa)
SEWA	Self-Employed Women's Association (India)
SHARE	Share Microfin Limited (India)
SHG	Self-help group
SIDA	Swedish International Development Agency
SIDBI	Small Indistrial Development Bank in India
TSKI	Taytay Sa Kauswagan, Inc. (Philippines)
UNCDF	United Nations Capital Development Fund
UNDP	United Nations Development Programme
UNIFEM	United Nations Development Fund for Women
USAID	United States Agency for International Development
WWB	Women's World Banking

1

Achieving the Microcredit Summit and Millennium Development Goals of Reducing Extreme Poverty: What Is the Cutting Edge on Cost-Effectively Measuring Movement across the $1/Day Threshold?

Thierry van Bastelaer and Manfred Zeller

INTRODUCTION

It is widely acknowledged that the majority of the world's population, mostly people in the developing world who live on less than $1 per day, do not have access to formal financial services. A recent World Bank study concluded that more than half of the poverty level reductions for poor clients in three Bangladeshi microfinance institutions (MFIs) could be directly attributed to microfinance. Its impact was greater on extreme poverty than on moderate poverty.[1]

In early 2005 the Microcredit Summit Campaign reaffirmed its commitment toward fulfilling the Millennium Development Goals—in particular, cutting the proportion of people living in absolute poverty in half by 2015. The campaign was also extended until 2015, with a focus on the following two goals:

- Ensuring that 175 million of the world's poorest families, especially the women of those families, will be receiving credit for self-employment and other financial and business services by the end of 2015

- Ensuring that by the end of 2015, 100 million of the world's poorest families will have sufficiently increased their incomes to exceed US$1 a day, adjusted for purchasing power parity (PPP)[2]

Both goals present a measurement challenge: the need for cost-effective tools that measure (1) whether a household lives on a per-capita income below US$1 a day and (2) whether household incomes move above US$1 a day per capita over time.

Microfinance organizations realize the importance of knowing more about their clients, particularly their poverty level. In parallel, policymakers, advocates, donors, and practitioners consider microfinance an effective step toward reaching the Millenium Development Goals, especially cutting poverty in half by 2015. A number of practitioner organizations have taken up the task of developing tools to assess the poverty level of their clients and to measure their movement out of poverty.

Adding to this momentum, in 2000 the U.S. Congress passed the Microenterprise for Self-Reliance Act, mandating that half of all United States Agency for International Development (USAID) microenterprise funds benefit the very poor. This act was amended in 2003. The lack of widely applicable, low-cost tools for assessing poverty based on absolute income makes it difficult for USAID to determine whether it is meeting these targets.[3] Therefore, the law requires USAID to develop and certify at least two tools for assessing the poverty level of its microenterprise beneficiaries.[4]

This mandate creates a unique opportunity to establish a basis for accurate yet simple quantitative measurements of poverty outreach, building on the accomplishments of microenterprise practitioners in this area. While very detailed and accurate tools—such as the World Bank's Living Standards Measurement Survey (LSMS)—are already available, they are time-consuming and expensive to implement. In addition, they are designed to be used by official statistical agencies over large, country-wide samples, rather than by practitioners interested in knowing the incidence of extreme poverty among their clients. Consequently, the last few years have seen a number of projects aimed at developing the means to accurately and easily measure the poverty outreach of microenterprise programs in relation to an absolute poverty line, such as $1/day. The resulting tools were designed for the specific needs of microenterprise practitioners with limited financial means, statistical expertise, and available staff.

This chapter describes the methodological challenges facing these efforts, how a team based at the IRIS Center at the University of Maryland chose to address these challenges under USAID funding, and what the IRIS findings suggest regarding the promises and obstacles confronting practitioners interested in measuring the poverty status of their clients and its change over time. Hence the chapter does not pretend to describe all possible approaches to measuring absolute poverty and tracking movement across the poverty line, nor to suggest that the IRIS approach is the only promising one. There are several groups currently working on this issue, and all of them face the same challenges. The aim of this chapter is to describe these common challenges and to suggest one possible way to address them.[5]

DEFINITIONS AND LIMITATIONS

The Microenterprise for Self-Reliance Act, as amended in 2003, defines the very poor as those individuals "living on less than the equivalent of a dollar a day" ($1.08 per day at 1993 PPP)—the definition of "extreme poverty" under the first Millennium Development Goal—or those individuals living in the bottom 50% below their country's poverty line.[6]

Most practitioners working in the field today know that poverty is much more than a household-level monetary measure of welfare. They see poverty as a multifaceted, complex phenomenon, some features of which are more relevant in certain situations than in others. Food security and access to public services, such as health care, water, sanitation, and education, while closely related to income, can have a major impact on poverty and hopelessness. Vulnerability to shocks affects the daily outlook of millions of families living close to subsistence levels. Participation in social activities or networks can provide a strong informal safety net. Household income levels above $1/day per capita can mask a very uneven distribution of income among household members, resulting in a disproportionate incidence of extreme poverty among women, children, and the elderly.

Some practitioner tools in development, such as those from Freedom from Hunger and FINCA, recognize the multidimensional character of poverty and explicitly include indicators of food security and social capital without necessarily linking them to specific income levels.

We join these and other groups in recognizing that poverty is too complex a concept to be reduced to a household's economic position in relation to an arbitrary income line. We also believe that more needs to be done toward understanding the poverty level of clients as defined through money-metric concepts used in the first Millenium Development Goal or by national governments. We therefore dedicate the rest of this chapter to a discussion of how the USAID/IRIS team addressed the specific challenges implicit in the Microenterprise for Self-Reliance Act, which define poverty in absolute terms and, more specifically, in relation to a national or international poverty line.

Relative measures can provide a critical dimension for measuring poverty. People's perception of their level of poverty is largely a function of how their situation compares with that of others in the same community. As research on happiness suggests, individuals who live on less than a dollar a day in the highlands of Peru can be more satisfied with their situation than, say, higher-earning industrial workers in Russia.[7]

Accordingly, most approaches that have been applied by practitioners have focused on measuring relative poverty. These include the social performance index by FINCA (Hatch 2002), the food security scales by Freedom from Hunger (MkNelly and Dunford 2002), and the tools developed by Opportunity International and the Trickle Up Program, as reviewed in Zeller (2004). Furthermore, many practitioners have used various location-specific housing or asset indices or employed the Participatory Wealth Ranking (Gibbons et al. 1999) for identifying the poor. The Consultative Group to Assist the Poor (CGAP) has developed and tested the Poverty Assessment Tool (PAT), which measures relative poverty using multidimensional indicators (Henry et al. 2003). In principle, all of these tools may be useful for targeting, and also for tracking shifts in the relative poverty status of clients over time, including the measurement of poverty's impact on a relative scale. However, at their current stage of practical implementation, these tools fail to predict whether a client's income places her below or above the national or international poverty line (or any other money-metric measure). It is therefore necessary to relate household poverty to specific standards and to develop and test tools that measure absolute poverty.

There are limits to what such tools can do. First, poverty tools cannot, by themselves, measure the impact of microfinance programs on poverty reduction and the contribution of the microfinance movement toward the achievement of the Millennium Development Goals (MDGs). Thus, we do not discuss various types of research designs for impact assessment. Nonetheless, since the tools can be used for tracking poverty over time in both client and nonclient households, they may possibly be used in the future for impact assessment.

Similarly, poverty tools cannot themselves testify as to the wider aspects of the "social performance" of microfinance institutions (MFIs) that go beyond poverty outreach or impact, nor can they assess the success of multi-fold strategies of MFIs in contributing to the MDG on poverty reduction.

Poverty tools can, however, under specific circumstances, measure the movement of groups of clients across the poverty line. This requires, first and foremost, the development of accurate and practical poverty tools. Once these are available and tested, their repeated use over time to track changes in poverty level poses no unusual conceptual or practical difficulty. The rest of this chapter therefore focuses on some of the issues that need to be addressed in the tool development process.

OVERVIEW OF THE IRIS APPROACH

The methodology selected by IRIS to develop tools that are as accurate as possible in addition to being easy and inexpensive to use revolves around two sequential series of tests: tests of accuracy, based on primary or secondary household expenditure data from twelve countries; and tests of practicality, run by microenterprise practitioners in fifteen countries. Allowing for separate tests ensures a controlled environment for testing accuracy that relies on rigorous data collection and statistical analysis, while also drawing on practitioner input for crucial information on the practicality of recommended tools. This double approach enables the tools to accurately report poverty levels while ensuring their ease of use at low cost to their ultimate users.

The *tests of accuracy* use primary and secondary data to identify sets of indicators that most accurately predict the poverty status of a randomly selected household. For the primary data collection, households in four countries across the four main USAID regions (Bangladesh, Peru, Uganda, and Kazakhstan) were surveyed by IRIS to test the predictive capacity of a variety of poverty measurement indicators. The second part of the accuracy analysis drew on preexisting Living Standards Measurement Survey (LSMS) data sets from an additional eight countries.[8] All countries were selected using a number of criteria, including the extent of USAID microenterprise funding, both globally and within each region; the intensity of microenterprise activities; the presence of preexisting expenditure data (such as that provided by LSMS, the Social Dimensions of Adjustment Integrated Survey [SDA-IS], or other survey including an expenditure module) for calibration of the poverty line; and geographic and linguistic variation. On the basis of this analysis, IRIS combined into six shortcut tools various combinations of those indicators that appeared most powerful at predicting extreme poverty in the twelve test countries.

As for the *tests of practicality*, local microenterprise practitioners implemented these shortcut tools to provide information about a variety of criteria, especially cost (in terms of time, money, infrastructure, etc.) and process/implementation issues. The IRIS team used a range of factors in assessing the tools for practicality:

- Which data collection methodologies work best for which types of practitioners

- Which indicators are easy and which are difficult to adapt, collect, and analyze

- How questionnaire length affects implementation

- How tools can be integrated into current data collection processes

- What level of expense is acceptable

- How staff can be adequately trained to implement the tools

- Which data entry techniques can be implemented for the tools

- What quality control measures will be necessary

- Management information system (MIS) requirements

The combination of accuracy and practicality data will result in a set of country-specific tools that will be considered by USAID for certification under the Microenterprise for Self-Reliance Act.

The remainder of this chapter describes the challenges faced in defining and improving the accuracy of the tools, and the solutions developed by the USAID/IRIS team. It also discusses the issues involved in testing accuracy on the basis of primary data, and the results of the tests in the twelve countries. A description of the practicality testing process and early results follows. After a note on the importance of gender considerations in poverty assessment, the analysis concludes with a discussion of the outlook for accurately measuring the movement of client groups across the $1/day poverty line.

HOW ACCURATE IS ACCURATE ENOUGH? DESCRIPTION AND RESULTS OF ACCURACY TESTS

From project inception, based on the available literature, the IRIS team suspected there would be a strong trade-off between accuracy and practicality. While not perfect, LSMS is probably the most accurate poverty assessment mechanism currently available, but its practicality is severely limited by the fact that its individual interviews last several hours and the data analysis requires advanced statistical and programming skills.

To a large extent, however, our results suggest that the accuracy of "shortcut" poverty assessment tools can be very close to that of LSMS with no marked limitations on their length, cost, or complexity. This observation appears to hold regardless of the degree of sophistication of the measure of accuracy employed. In this section we examine what accuracy is, why it matters, and how it can be measured.

The accuracy of poverty assessment tools can be measured using two main ratios:

- The proportion of clients whose poverty status—"very poor" or "not very-poor"—is correctly assessed (i.e., the "very poor" correctly identified as such, plus the "not very-poor" correctly identified as such). This proportion is known as *total accuracy.*[9]

- The proportion of "very poor" clients who are correctly assessed, known as *poverty accuracy.*

Both of these measures can be useful, although for the specific purposes of the legislation, USAID is more likely to be interested in how correctly the tools assess the poverty level of the very poor (the second ratio above) rather than that of the very poor *and* the not very-poor (the first ratio above). Hence the IRIS tools place more importance on the second ratio.

Given the purpose of the legislation, however, there is another measure that is important for USAID: the proportion of clients whose actual poverty status is incorrectly classified. Indeed, since Congress's intent is to ensure that 50% of microenterprise funding is targeted at the very poor, it is important to minimize the number of the very poor who are not reached by microenterprise programs because they are incorrectly classified as not very-poor (known as *undercoverage error*) and also to minimize the number of not very-poor who benefit from these programs because they have been erroneously classified as very poor (*leakage error*).[10]

It is therefore critical to develop poverty assessment tools that correctly identify and minimize classification errors. Equally important is the extent to which the tools can balance the two types of error. Since the congressional requirement relates to the poverty level of *groups* of clients—as opposed to *individual* clients—the fact that a large number of very poor clients are incorrectly classified as not very-poor is of little concern if that figure is equal to the number of not very-poor clients misclassified as very poor.[11] Consider the case of a tool that is used to report on the number of very poor clients in a group of ten. If the tool incorrectly classifies four very poor clients as not very-poor, and four not very-poor clients as very poor, the errors cancel out and don't affect the aggregate result. If the tool, however, is used for individual assessment (or targeting), the errors *add up*: eight people have been incorrectly identified, with the result that four very poor clients may not receive the services designed for them, while four not very-poor clients may receive services for which their poverty status does not qualify them.

Based on IRIS's recommendations, USAID decided to use as a measure of accuracy a criterion that was developed specifically for this project and that takes into account the preference for balanced errors in addition to the poverty accuracy produced by the tools. This indicator—the Balanced Poverty

Accuracy Criterion (BPAC)—is computed as poverty accuracy minus the absolute difference between undercoverage and leakage, each expressed as a percentage of the total number of very poor.[12] Using this new composite measure of accuracy, IRIS implemented a statistical analysis that resulted in sets of indicators that identified the very poor in the twelve project countries, while ensuring in most cases that the errors are perfectly balanced. The challenges and results of this analysis are presented in the next section.

Approach

A research protocol was developed for the four countries where primary data collection was undertaken (Bangladesh, Peru, Uganda, and Kazakhstan). The survey consisted of two modules: a composite survey questionnaire containing a broad array of multidimensional poverty indicators, and a benchmark questionnaire for measurement of absolute poverty. The composite survey questionnaire was compiled from several existing practitioner tools and the poverty literature, and was administered in the first visit to the sample of 800 households in each country.

The composite survey is not, per se, a prototype of the tool(s) that IRIS recommended to USAID for certification in September 2006, but a "tool incubator" through which a large number of combinations of practitioner indicators may be tested for accuracy. The composite survey allowed the team, which was faced with strict time constraints resulting from the implementation deadlines of the legislation, to test large numbers of indicators developed by practitioners without having to test the complete preexisting tools in a large number of countries.

The benchmark questionnaire for measuring the absolute poverty of sample households (i.e., the "true" poverty status) was developed using a modified version of the expenditure module of the LSMS.[13] Using this questionnaire, detailed expenditure data were collected from the same sample of households in each country, exactly fourteen days after the first visit, to provide the best available quantitative information on the "true" poverty status of each household. The two-week interval created a bounded-recall situation (involving such questions as "Since our last visit, how much rice did you buy?") that increased the accuracy of the comparison with the responses to benchmark survey. Statistical methods were then used to identify the fifteen indicators within the composite survey that most accurately predict the "true" poverty status of the households—that is, that most closely track the benchmark results.

Sampling, Poverty Rates, and Poverty Lines

In Bangladesh, Peru, Kazakhstan, and Uganda, IRIS performed accuracy tests involving primary data collection in collaboration with experienced local survey firms. The tasks of the survey firms were to adapt the generic composite survey questionnaire as well as the benchmark questionnaire to the national and local contexts and to carry out nationally representative surveys of 800 households.[14] Data cleaning and analysis were performed by the Institute of Rural Development at the University of Göttingen, Germany, and IRIS.

In the analysis, a household was classified as "very poor" if either (a) the household was "living on less than the equivalent of a dollar a day per capita" ($1.08 per day at 1993 PPP)—the international definition of "extreme poverty" under the Millennium Development Goals ("international poverty line")—or (b) the household was among the poorest 50% percent of households below the country's own national poverty line ("national poverty line"). The proportion of the population classified as "very poor" in these four countries, and the specific poverty line against which they were computed, are shown in Table 1.1.

The use of both poverty definitions in the accuracy tests leads to time-consuming calculations. The calculation of the international $1 per day poverty line (actually $1.08 per day, based on 1993 prices) requires a conversion with the PPP rate to reflect the equivalent purchasing power in local currency at the time of the survey. In Bangladesh, $1.08 was worth 23.18 taka at the time of the accuracy survey in March 2004. In comparison, the market exchange rate during the same month was around 60 taka per U.S. dollar, suggesting that the lack of correction for PPP would have resulted in a significant overcounting of very poor clients.[15]

The identification of the very poor using the concept of the bottom 50% below the national poverty line is equally cumbersome, for a number of reasons. Some countries have no official poverty line, while others use several of them to reflect differences in prices and living costs across regions. For example, in Peru and Kazakhstan there are seven and fourteen poverty lines, respectively. While the regional poverty lines are published in Peru and Kazakhstan, the median per-capita daily expenditures for identifying the bottom 50% of households below the national poverty line are not. Hence, the only way to accurately quantify the median per-capita daily expenditures for households below the regional poverty line—a necessary first step in identifying households in the bottom 50% below the poverty line—is to have direct access to nationally representative household expenditure data from each of the regions. The difficulties with this approach relate to data access and to the time involved in calculating inflation-adjusted median per-capita daily expenditures for each of the regions.

Table 1.1   Poverty Incidence by Country

Country	Poverty Rate (%)	Poverty Line Used
Bangladesh	31.40	International
Peru	26.88	National
Uganda	32.36	International
Kazakhstan	4.53	National

Source: Calculations described in Zeller et al. (2005a, 2005b, 2005c, 2005d).

POVERTY OUTREACH OF MICROFINANCE INSTITUTIONS IN FOUR COUNTRIES

Data collection for the accuracy tests in Bangladesh, Peru, Kazakhstan, and Uganda had the additional benefit of allowing the calculation of the poverty outreach of financial institutions whose clients were included in the random samples in these countries. As the data are derived from nationally representative samples, the samples include not only entering clients, but all types of clients of financial institutions. Table 1.2 shows the results of these calculations. Among the four countries, Bangladesh had the highest breadth of outreach. Forty-three percent of households in the nationally representative sample were clients of financial institutions. With respect to depth of outreach (as measured by the percentage of very poor among the clients), Bangladesh dominates the other countries by a wide margin, with about 30% of clients classified as very poor. In the other three countries, the breadth and depth of outreach of microfinance institutions are much lower. These striking differences appear largely due to the strong poverty targeting focus and extensive outreach of microfinance institutions that have been established over the last three decades in densely populated Bangladesh. The very low depth of outreach in Kazakhstan can be explained by the fact that only 4.5% of households in the national sample are very poor and that most clients are relatively wealthy savers using commercial or state-owned banks instead of microfinance institutions.

Table 1.2   Poverty Outreach of Financial Institutions in Four Countries

Country	Breadth of Outreach (Percent of Clients in Total Population)	Depth of Outreach (Percent of Very Poor out of Total Clients)	Percent of Clients Below $1/day Poverty Line (at PPP Rates)
Bangladesh	43.2	30.4	30.4
Kazakhstan	13.3	0.90	<0.9
Peru	6.9	11.25	2.5
Uganda	5.1	15.00	15.0

Note: For Kazakhstan, clients of business development institutions are included in the figures. For Peru, the basis for the percentage calculation is the number of adult persons; for all other countries, the basis is number of households.

Table 1.3   Depth of Poverty Outreach in Bangladesh, by Type of Financial Institution

Type of Financial Institution	Mean of Per-Capita Daily Expenditures (Taka)	Percentage of Households Below $1/Day per Capita (PPP Rates)
Top 45 NGOs and Grameen Bank	29.89	44.38
Other NGOs and civic institutions	42.89	11.11
Public banks or government credit programs	43.65	17.97
Privately owned banks, cooperatives, or other institutions, excluding Grameen Bank	34.60	25.00
Total clients (n = 345)	36.50	30.43

Source: Zeller et al. (2005a), Table 5.3.1.

Given the high number of clients in the nationally representative sample in Bangladesh, an additional detailed analysis of depth of outreach, differentiated by type of financial institutions, may be performed (see Table 1.3).

The top forty-five microfinance NGOs and Grameen Bank are reaching the very poor in relatively high numbers, as 44% of all of their clients live below the international poverty line. Actually, this figure likely underestimates the true poverty outreach of MFIs because many clients may have moved out of poverty by the time of the survey.[16]

IDENTIFICATION OF SETS OF POVERTY INDICATORS

This section briefly describes the statistical analysis that leads to the identification of the five, ten, and fifteen indicators that most accurately reflect the "true" poverty status of a household—that is, that most closely track the observed poverty status as measured by the benchmark questionnaire. To identify powerful poverty indicators, IRIS estimated several types of regression models in each of the twelve study countries.[17] The purpose of these analyses was to use information collected on a large number of indicators to predict the observed per-capita daily expenditures and, by comparing these expenditures with the appropriate poverty line, to predict the poverty status of a household.[18]

In all twelve countries, one standard set of regressors was defined that included variables usually contained in the LSMS. These regressors include poverty indicators mainly related to demography, possession of assets, housing characteristics, education, and occupation. In the four countries with primary data collection, it was possible to define eight additional sets of regressors from the composite survey questionnaire that incorporated many more dimensions of poverty, such as social capital, food security and vulnerability, access to finance, and exposure to risks. These larger sets of indicators led to the identification of poverty assessment tools with somewhat higher-accuracy performance. There is a double trade-off, however. First, these indicators are available only in the few countries where they have been gathered by practitioners, which limits their usefulness in developing tools for a larger number of countries. Second, the larger sets of regressors also contain more complex indicators, such as the value of food expenditures in the past month or the area of agricultural land owned by the household. Such variables are obviously more difficult to elicit in an interview, compared with, for example, the simple observation of the type of roof on the household's residence.

Table 1.4 shows the levels of accuracy reached by the tools generated by IRIS in twelve nationally representative samples. Note that the accuracy of the tools declines markedly when the prevalence of poverty is lower. This should not be surprising: the rarer a phenomenon, the more difficult it is to accurately capture its incidence. In practical terms, this means that a very poor household in Kazakhstan is much less likely to be classified correctly than a very poor household in India.

Table 1.4   Accuracy Results in the Twelve Test Countries

Country	Poverty Incidence (%)	Total Accuracy	Poverty Accuracy	Under-coverage Error	Leakage Error	BPAC	PIE
Kazakhstan	4.52	94.61	40.54	59.46	59.46	40.54	0.00
Jamaica	8.03	92.85	54.69	45.31	43.75	53.13	–0.13
Albania	10.42	90.21	53.97	46.03	47.94	52.06	0.20
Ghana	13.42	87.51	53.90	46.10	46.95	53.05	0.11
Vietnam	14.52	91.61	71.66	28.34	29.50	70.50	0.17
Guatemala	22.96	88.16	74.10	25.90	25.66	73.86	–0.06
Peru	26.88	85.13	72.56	27.44	27.91	72.09	0.13
Bangladesh	31.41	83.48	74.50	25.50	27.09	72.98	0.50
Loan size tool		68.11	15.23	84.76	20.00	–49.53	–19.68
Uganda	32.36	79.06	67.84	32.16	32.55	67.45	0.13
Madagascar	35.22	84.85	78.61	21.39	21.62	78.38	0.08
Tajikistan	47.29	73.45	71.93	28.07	28.07	71.93	0.00
India (UP and Bihar)	77.87	86.50	91.33	8.67	8.67	91.33	0.00

Notes: Results were taken from the highest-performing statistical method for each country. The loan size tool was tested only in Bangladesh.
Source: IRIS, final accuracy results, as summarized in http://www.povertytools.org/Project_Documents/Accuracy%20Results%20for%2012%20Countries.pdf.

Most significant for the purpose of the poverty assessment legislation, the best statistical models are those that select sets of indicators that equalize the two types of errors: the proportion of very poor clients misclassified as not very-poor (undercoverage) is equal—or very close—to the proportion of not very-poor clients incorrectly classified as very poor (leakage).

One way to judge the performance of these new tools is to compare their accuracy against that of an existing indicator of depth of outreach, such as loan size. In the case of Bangladesh, where the sample included the largest proportion of microfinance clients, an analysis of the accuracy of loan size as a predictor of per-capita daily expenditures, and therefore poverty status, was possible. As shown in Table 1.4, undercoverage error exceeds 80% with the best-calibrated loan size tool, indicating that more than four out of five very poor households in the Bangladesh sample are wrongly predicted as not very-poor by the loan size indicator. Using loan size as a predictor of poverty can clearly lead to high levels of misclassification, especially among the very poor.

POVERTY INDICATORS FOR TWELVE PROJECT COUNTRIES

Three main results emerge from the analysis of accuracy described above. First, the same small number of indicator categories contain the best predictors of poverty status in most of the countries in the analysis. In all countries, per-capita daily expenditure on clothing was selected as a powerful predictor of poverty status. In nine of the twelve countries, housing indicators were important predictors of extreme poverty. Other powerful categories of indicators include education, durables, and assets. Second, within each of these categories, the specific indicators that best predict poverty, as well as their weights, vary significantly from country to country. For example, a specific type of asset that accurately predicts poverty in Bangladesh—such as the gender of the head of household—may be different from the one that effectively identifies a poor household in Kazakhstan—such as the level of primary education of household members. Finally, relatively high levels of accuracy can be reached with the use of a fairly small number of indicators, and the benefit of including additional indicators in the poverty tools is increasingly lower in terms of accuracy. Table 1.5 lists the indicators that appeared among the top fifteen in at least three of the twelve country studies.

HOW PRACTICAL IS PRACTICAL ENOUGH? EARLY LESSONS FROM PRACTICALITY TESTS

One of the most innovative aspects of the Microenterprise for Self-Reliance Act is the requirement that tools be designed for use by practitioners as opposed to survey firms or government statistical offices. This specification offers a number of unique opportunities, such as the possibility for practitioners to (1) increase their knowledge of the circumstances facing their clients and (2) use this information to refine the design and features of their products and services. It also presents a set of challenges, such as maintaining quality control, combining data collection with staff's existing duties, and managing strategic behavior by clients and staff.

To learn more about these opportunities and challenges, IRIS organized a series of practicality tests, funded by USAID and implemented in the fall of 2005 and the spring of 2006 by fourteen microenterprise practitioner organizations in fifteen countries.[19]

Table 1.5   Most Powerful Poverty Indicators in the Twelve Project Countries

	Poverty Incidence Lower than 20%					Poverty Incidence Greater than 20%							
	KZ	JA	AL	GH	VN	GT	PE	BA	UG	MD	TJ	IN	Total
Clothing expenditures	x	x	x	x	x	x	x	x	x	x	x	x	12
Household members: no education		x		x	x	x		x	x			x	7
House size: number of rooms		x	x	x		x				x		x	6
Refrigerator	x	x	x	x	x						x		6
Household members: incomplete primary education	x	x			x	x						x	5
Car		x	x	x		x					x		5
Radio				x	x					x	x	x	5
Stove		x		x	x	x					x		5
Female household head		x		x				x		x	x		5
Number of cows owned	x			x				x			x	x	5
Household members: complete primary education		x	x	x		x							4
Household members: incomplete secondary education	x	x				x			x				4
Household head: university education		x	x		x						x		4
Phone		x	x				x				x		4
Television					x	x				x	x		4
Sent remittances as proportion of income	x						x	x			x		4

Country abbreviations: Albania (AL), Bangladesh (BA), Ghana (GH), Guatemala (GT), India (IN, Uttar Pradesh and Bihar only), Jamaica (JA), Kazakhstan (KZ), Madagascar (MD), Peru (PE), Tajikistan (TJ), Uganda (UG), Vietnam (VN).

The dual purpose of the tests was to (1) learn how specific indicators performed during the tests, so that the most sensitive, difficult-to-understand, and time-consuming ones can be considered for exclusion from the final tools; and (2) identify the practical implementation issues that USAID may want to consider as part of its tool certification process.

Although final results from the practicality tests are only beginning to emerge as of this writing, a number of broad lessons are already clear:

1. Tools can be short and simple to apply.

Most shortcut tools can be implemented by practitioners in a client interview that lasts less than fifteen minutes, to which the time for data entry and analysis back at headquarters needs to be added. The shortest tools can take as little as 10 minutes, and only those that collect detailed household information require more than 20 minutes of the client's time.

2. Enlist vigorous management support.

One unambiguous lesson is that support from local and headquarters management is absolutely critical to the success of poverty assessment activities. Enthusiasm, intellectual leadership, motivation, and active encouragement by management at every stage of the poverty assessment program is essential for ensuring that an activity is efficient and fulfilling for staff and clients, and generates information useful to the organization in addition to the sponsor.

3. Manage client and staff incentives.

One of the explicit or implicit purposes of poverty assessment is to increase practitioners' knowledge of their clients' needs and to improve the nature or delivery of products. Not surprisingly, however, if clients are aware that their answers have the potential to influence the selection of products that are available to them, they face an incentive to provide answers that exaggerate or—less often—understate their poverty level.

In addition, to the extent that practitioners wish to demonstrate the incidence of extreme poverty among their clients, another layer of incentives enters into play: staff may be tempted to overstate the proportion of very poor households in the groups with which they work.[20]

An accurate representation of poverty outreach numbers among microenterprise clients therefore requires a clear incentive structure for clients, and for staff if they perceive that their performance evaluation is affected by the reported extent of poverty among their clients. Some recommendations from the practicality tests are presented next.

At the client level:

- The timing of the poverty interview is critical. If poverty tools are applied at the time of loan application, clients may be tempted to adjust their responses to make them eligible for the loan. It is therefore strongly advised that poverty data be gathered after loan decisions have been made—for example, at the time of loan disbursement.

- Clients need to know that their answers don't affect access to products. Even if poverty interviews do not take place at the time of loan application, clients may have motives to appear poorer (or richer) than they actually are. Clients therefore need to be informed that their answers will have no bearing on their future access to products and services.

- Location of the interview can affect the verifiability of answers. To the extent possible, interviews should take place in the client's home—rather than at the NGO's facility or the meeting place—so that the client's answers to housing- and asset-related questions can be visually verified by the interviewer.

At the staff level:

- Accuracy matters more than the number of very poor clients reported. The staff must be convinced that the accuracy of their reporting is more important for the purposes of poverty assessment than the actual number of clients who are reported as very poor.

- To the extent possible, the design of the tool should not allow the interviewer to predict or affect the poverty score of individual clients, to avoid tempting them to manipulate answers to produce a specific result. Scores should either be hidden from staff or computed electronically when data on all clients have been collected.[21]

4. Weigh the pluses and minuses of outsourcing poverty assessment.

Most practitioners involved in the practicality testing of the tools indicated that they intend to outsource to local survey firms or research outfits the task of collecting poverty outreach data for reporting to USAID. These organizations prefer to ask survey professionals or university students to obtain poverty data from their clients rather than adding this task to their staff's already full schedules, aware as they are that the preexisting relationship between clients and staff may lead to a more truthful and cooperative experience.

IRIS's observations in the field do not suggest that outsourcing is incompatible with well-run and useful poverty assessment activities. Provided that local and headquarters management is fully on board and supportive, involving carefully selected and trained survey professionals can help ensure that data are collected and analyzed correctly. On the other end of the spectrum, overworked practitioner staff or insufficiently experienced outside researchers may not be able to adequately implement all of the steps involved in measuring client poverty, which may have a significant impact on the quality of the data and on the value of the exercise to the organization itself.

5. Provide constant quality control.

Whether or not the decision is made to outsource the poverty assessment of its clients to professional survey firms or research groups, an organization needs to commit significant time and resources to enforce strict quality control. Although the tools themselves are simple to implement, the overall exercise requires careful planning, adequate training, hands-on practice, proper implementation—particularly in the areas of sampling, probing, thoroughness, and accuracy—and constant attention to detail.

GENDER AND POVERTY MEASUREMENT

Practitioners are well aware that the distribution of income, resources, and power is rarely equitable within households. The combined effects of cultural influences that put a premium on male welfare and leadership and of microenterprise programs that are generally directed at women creates a very wide space for discrepancy in the distribution of income and power within households. Without an understanding of the structures of power and the degree of intra-household transfers, it remains challenging to confirm the widespread impression that women confront a higher level of poverty than men living in the same household.

The USAID/IRIS project explored early the availability of simple, inexpensive, off-the-shelf methods to capture differences in absolute poverty among members of the same household. Although no such methodology was found at the time, the project is dedicated to contributing to future efforts in this area, and a gender expert is currently working to provide the conceptual direction for this effort.

To add existing gender knowledge to the current project, practitioners involved in the practicality tests were trained in incorporating gender concerns in the implementation of the draft tools.

WHAT DO SHORTCUT TOOLS LOOK LIKE?

Figure 1.1 shows a possible format for the USAID/IRIS tool. The specific nature and order of the questions will be determined for each tool that is certified for use in a specific country.[22]

WHAT IS THE OUTLOOK FOR MEASURING MOVEMENT ACROSS THE $1/DAY THRESHOLD?

What does the preceding discussion teach us about the ability of shortcut poverty tools to measure the movement of very poor households out of "extreme poverty," as defined by the Millennium Development Goals (across the $1.08 per day line, measured at 1993 PPP)? Although our answer to this question is based on our own experiences with the USAID/IRIS tools, we note that the following arguments are in line with lessons from other tool development projects.

Although they are generally designed to produce "snapshot" assessments of poverty outreach, shortcut tools can be used to measure movement across the $1/day line, provided that all of the following conditions are met:

- The poverty line is expressed in terms of PPP rather than the market exchange rate.

- Tools are calibrated for the country to which they are applied.

- Tools are kept up to date between the first and the last measurements.

- Poverty status is assessed on groups of clients.

- Respondents are entering clients at the time of first measurement.

- Poverty data are collected at regular intervals on the same sample of clients.

The rest of this section examines these conditions in order.

Figure 1.1 USAID/IRIS Poverty Assessment Tool—Draft

SURVEY NUMBER: _____

Supervisor QC Date	_____	Initials _____
Head Quarters QC Date	_____	Initials _____
MIS Data Entry Date	_____	Initials _____

Enterprise Type: _____

1. Manufacturing
2. Trade or Retail
3. Food Services
4. Transport
5. Other Services
6. Agric/Animals
7. Fishing
8. Other

Date of Interview _____

Start Time _____

Interviewer (code) _____

Sex of Interviewer [ ] 0=Female; 1=Male

Branch (code) _____

Time in Program _____ Months

Client Type _____

Region/ Dept. _____

Client Location [ ] 1. Urban; 2. Semi-urban; 3. Rural

Figure 1.1 USAID/IRIS Poverty Assessment Tool—Draft (Continued)

1. Client or ID # _____   2. Group # _____

Instructions: Ask the client the questions exactly as they are written below, and in the same order. Indicate answers in the boxes to the right of the questions.

Interviewer: Say: "Hello. My name is _____. I work for the organization _____. We are trying to learn a little bit more about the clients we work with, and so I have a few questions I'd like to ask today. It should only take us about 15 minutes, and the answers you provide will be put together with answers from ___ (#) other households. All of your answers are completely confidential and your name will not be given with your answers. Are you willing to take some time to answer these questions today?"

3. What is
   your age?

4. Sex:

   Observe, don't ask.
   0=Female; 1=Male.

5. What is your marital status? *(read responses; enter only one code in box)*

1. *Married or living together;* 2. *Married but living separately;* 3. *Single;* 4. *Divorced/Separated;* 5. *Widowed*

Interviewer: Say: "I would like to ask you some questions about the people in your household. Let me tell you a little bit about what we mean by 'household.' For the purpose of this survey, a household is a single person, or a group of people who live under the same roof, combine their incomes and assets, and eat from the same pot. A household member is someone who has lived in the household for at least 6 months over the last year." Answer any questions. Refer to the Implementer's Guide if you have any questions. Refer to the Implementer's Guide before proceeding.

6. According to this definition, how many people live in your household?

Interviewer: Ask the respondent who is the main income earner in the household. Refer to the Implementer's Guide if you have any questions.

Figure 1.1 USAID/IRIS Poverty Assessment Tool—Draft (Continued)

7. Who is the main income earner in the household throughout the year?

☐ 0=Respondent;
1=Other

Interviewer: Only inquire about sex and age if the respondent is NOT the main income earner.

Interviewer: Say: "I have a few questions about this person." NOTE: If respondent IS the main income earner, modify questions accordingly.

Sex: ☐ 0=Female;
1=Male

Age: ☐

8. What is the highest level of education achieved by the main income earner?

☐

*Enter highest grade level passed/completed; for example, if currently in 8, then 7 is highest completed.
(completed primary=6; completed secondary=10; higher secondary certificate=12; BA/BS=14; MA=16; PhD=18)*

Interviewer: Only ask the following two questions if the respondent's level of education is less than 14.

9. Can the main income earner read a complete sentence?

☐ 0=no, 1=yes

10. Can the main income earner write a complete sentence?

☐ 0=no, 1=yes

11. In the past 12 months, how many days have you been ill and unable to participate in normal daily activity?

☐

12. In the past 12 months, how many members of your household have been ill and unable to participate in normal daily activity?

Interviewer: Say: "I also have a few questions about your home."

Figure 1.1   USAID/IRIS Poverty Assessment Tool—Draft (Continued)

13. In your house, on what do you sleep?
    1=Floor; 2=Thin sleeping mat made of natural fibers; 3=Thin sleeping mat made of industrial fibers; 4=Thick mattress made of natural fibers; 5=Thick mattress made of industrial fibers; 6=Bed

14. What has been the total of all clothing and footwear expenses in your household for the last 12 months?
    *Note: If sewn at home, ask the respondent to estimate the cost of purchasing a similar item.

Interviewer: Say: "Now I would like to ask you a few questions about some items that are present in your house and some of the tools that you use in your agricultural business."
    Note: If you are using visual illustrations, show them to the respondent now.

15. Does your household own any type of audio equipment?

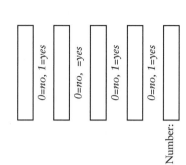

    0=no, 1=yes

16. Does your household own a camera?

    0=no, =yes

17. Does your household own a rickshaw?

    0=no, 1=yes

18. Does your household own a thresher?

    0=no, 1=yes

19. How many pigs does your household own?   Number:

20. Does your household own any tractors?   What is their current total value?
    Number: Value:

Figure 1.1 USAID/IRIS Poverty Assessment Tool—Draft (Continued)

21. What is the total value of all dishes owned by your household?   Value: ☐

22. What is the total value of all metal pots owned by your household?   Value: ☐

23. What is the total area of all land owned by your household?   ☐

Interviewer: Say: "I have one question about money being sent from abroad, which I know may be sensitive. I assure you that the answers will not be shared with anybody else."

24. During the last 12 months, has some member of your family working somewhere else or in another country
(i.e., not a household member at present!) or any friends of the family sent you money?   ☐   0=no, 1=yes
If yes, proceed to question 25. If no, proceed to the end.

25. Please estimate the proportion of your household's total income over the last 12 months that was received from elsewhere.   ☐ %

Interviewer: Look over the survey to see if you have missed any questions. If you have, please ask those questions of the respondent. If not, the interview is complete. Remember to thank the respondent for his/her time in helping you to answer these questions!

The Poverty Line Is Expressed in PPP Terms

As described for the Bangladesh data collection, ensuring that the purchasing power parity exchange rate is used to express the poverty line in local currency is a critical element in accurately measuring $1/day poverty (as defined in the Millenium Development Goals) and its movement across that line. In almost all developing and transition economies, market exchange rates are significantly higher than their PPP equivalents. In Cambodia, for example, the average market exchange rate as of January 2006 was 4,119 riels per dollar, whereas the PPP rate for the most recent prices was only 892 riels per dollar. Similarly, in Ethiopia the average market exchange rate as of January 2006 was 8.6 birrs per dollar, while the PPP exchange rate yielded no more than 1.97 birrs per dollar. In the Kyrgyz Republic, the market and PPP rates as of January 2005 were, respectively, 41 and 15 soms per dollar. In these three countries, as in most others, the use of the market exchange rate to determine a poverty line would result in grossly exaggerated poverty outreach numbers and in an inaccurate assessment of the number of clients moving across the poverty line.[23]

Tools Are as Accurate as Is Technically Feasible

Although the very nature of the exercise and the current methodological advances means that no poverty assessment tool can be perfectly accurate, the precision of the measurement across the poverty line is critically dependent on the accuracy of the poverty tool used. This accuracy—as measured by the Balanced Poverty Accuracy Criterion (BPAC)—is highest when the following two factors are combined:

- Poverty accuracy is maximized: the largest possible number of very poor clients are correctly predicted as such by the tool.

- Undercoverage and leakage errors are of the same magnitude: the number of very poor clients incorrectly included among the not very-poor is the same as the number of not very-poor clients erroneously predicted as very poor (each expressed as a proportion of the total number of very poor clients).

As described earlier in the chapter, this accuracy is affected by a number of factors, the most important one being the incidence of poverty in the country or region under analysis: if extreme poverty is relatively rare, the ability of any tool to assess it accurately is diminished. There are, however, two possible ways for practitioners to be confident that the tools they are using are as accurate as possible given poverty incidence and the methodological processes at their disposal. The first is to establish a minimum acceptable level for BPAC in each country where the tool is implemented; any tool that does not reach this minimum level is rejected for purposes of the measurement. The second approach is for the practitioner to require the tool developer to demonstrate that the statistical method chosen to select the indicators and weights included in the tool yields a higher BPAC than any of the other available methods. This approach presents the advantage that tools are selected only on the basis of how they perform compared with alternative statistical methods for the same country data; it does not penalize tools that result in low accuracy simply because they were developed for countries with low poverty incidence.

Tools Are Calibrated for the Country Where They Are Applied

Absolute poverty tools currently available combine indicators and weights identified through data analysis from specific countries, and they will reach the highest levels of accuracy in these countries. While there is no technical reason to avoid the use of these tools in assessing the poverty of groups of clients in other countries, it should be expected that country-specific tools will perform very inaccurately in countries for which they have not been calibrated.

The reason for this is that indicators that are closely linked to poverty status in one country may either not be applicable in other countries (such as a rickshaw in Russia or a pig in Pakistan) or have a very different relationship to poverty in these countries (e.g., the type of cooking fuel is a strong indicator of poverty in Bangladesh, but not in Albania.)

What can practitioners do if they are interested in measuring poverty in countries for which no absolute poverty tools have been developed? The first possible solution involves developing "international tools" that could be applied in any country. IRIS developed two such tools (the first one based on the poorest countries in our sample of twelve, and the second one based on the relatively less poor countries in the sample), and noted that these tools are significantly less accurate than country-specific tools.[24] Even if they had been sufficiently accurate, the amount of data and analysis necessary to adjust the international tools to each country's characteristics would be equivalent to that needed to develop a country-specific tool, which is likely to be much more accurate in any case. Hence, international tools appear to be both inaccurate and inefficient. The best solution is therefore to develop a tool for each country, a conclusion that Grameen Foundation and ACCION, among others, have also reached as part of their own poverty outreach analyses.

Developing country-specific tools requires detailed household expenditure data. For the twelve countries included in the IRIS/USAID project, these data were provided by field surveys in four countries and by LSMS data for the other eight countries. Developing tools for a larger number of countries necessitates access to household expenditure data collected as part of LSMS or Social Dimension of Adjustment (SDA) surveys, or from expenditure surveys conducted by individual countries' statistical agencies.[25] Should any of these data sources be found to be outdated, unavailable, or unreliable, primary data collection—such as the two-part composite plus expenditure benchmark surveys conducted by IRIS in Bangladesh, Kazakhstan, Peru, and Uganda—is necessary. Tools can then be designed for each country for which these data are available.

Tools Are Kept Up to Date between the First and Last Measurements

Just as tools must be adjusted to capture economic differences between countries, they need to be able to capture economic changes over time within countries. Changing economic conditions in a country typically affect the identification and importance of those indicators that best predict poverty. This means that in order to provide accurate results at different points in time, tools need to be adjusted—every few years in case of slow economic development, and more frequently in case of significant growth and poverty reduction—on the basis of up-to-date household expenditure data.[26]

Poverty Status Is Assessed on Groups of Clients

As described earlier, errors in poverty assessment are of two types: misclassifying a very poor household as not very-poor (undercoverage error); and misclassifying a not very-poor household as very poor (leakage error). Over a large enough sample, individual misclassifications should be of little concern to practitioners—provided the two types of error *cancel each other out*.[27] As described in this paper, statistical techniques are available to identify sets and weights of indicators that result, in most cases, in balanced errors. Even if balanced over a large sample, however, errors matter very much at the individual level, since they add up instead of canceling each other out. This explains why the same tool can be very accurate for measuring poverty at a collective level, but very inaccurate if used on an individual basis.[28]

Respondents Are Entering Clients at the Time of First Measurement

In order not to penalize programs that have been successful at moving their clients out of poverty, the sample for measuring changes in poverty outreach should be constituted exclusively of entering clients, which generally refers to clients who joined the program during the previous six months and, ideally, have not yet received a loan. This is the approach advocated by, among others, the CGAP Poverty Assessment Tool (Henry et al. 2003).

Poverty Data Are Collected at Regular Intervals on the Same Sample of Clients

This requirement is relatively straightforward. Once a sample of clients has been identified, its members will be visited on a regular—preferably yearly—basis, and data collected from them will be used to calculate the change in the proportion of clients falling below the appropriate poverty line. Although it will not accurately track the movement of specific clients across this line, the evolution of this data over time will allow for a reliable indication of the number of clients who have moved out of extreme poverty.

CONCLUSION

Thanks to the efforts of field researchers and practitioners over the last few years, poverty assessment is no longer the exclusive territory of large statistical agencies and research bureaus. The work of IRIS, Grameen Foundation USA, ACCION, and others has shown that absolute income poverty can be assessed at relatively low cost and with high levels of accuracy compared with the expensive and time-consuming LSMS method. This chapter has detailed the approach chosen by the IRIS team to address the challenges inherent in the congressional mandate, and the solutions it has devised to design accurate yet simple tools to measure the poverty level of groups of microenterprise clients.

The first main result from this project is that the same broad categories of indicators accurately predict poverty rates in many areas of the developing world, although the specific indicators and their weights vary significantly from country to country. Additionally, the tools are most accurate in those countries where poverty incidence is the highest. As mandated under the very specific requirements of the US legislation, the tools are designed to measure poverty rates in groups of clients. Their high level of performance is partly the result of a conscious choice not to require the tools to perform additional duties, such as individual assessment and targeting. Tracking the movement of sufficiently large groups of clients across a poverty line is made possible by the tools, provided that they are calibrated within countries and over time.

The second main result is that, although the tools themselves are short and simple to apply, their correct implementation requires significant commitment and attention to the practical aspects of data collection and analysis—particularly engagement by the organization's leadership, the structure of incentives for both clients and staff, careful decisions about outsourcing, and constant attention to quality control.

We believe that, thanks to tools such as those described in this chapter, microenterprise practitioners are now better equipped to meet the requirements of the US legislation, and we hope that the tools will also help them meet broader goals, to ultimately better serve the very poor. Ongoing efforts in the development of poverty assessment tools may provide critical inputs for microenterprise practitioners to better target the poor, innovate in developing and providing pro-poor products and services, and strengthen their impact on sustainable poverty reduction.[29]

Notes

1. Khandker, Shahidur R. "Microfinance and Poverty: Evidence Using Panel Data from Bangladesh." *World Bank Economic Review* 19(2), 2005.
2. Assuming an average of five per family, this goal would mean that 500 million people would have risen above US$1 a day, nearly completing the Millennium Development Goal of halving absolute poverty.
3. Currently, USAID's measure of poverty outreach for its microenterprise clients is loan size. Congressional action was in part motivated by the widespread realization that the dynamics of microenterprise development are too complex to suggest that there is a simple and reliable correlation between the size of a client's loan and her poverty level—especially if the nature of the support is focused on business development services rather than microfinance.
4. A "poverty assessment tool" for the purpose of this paper encompasses, in addition to a set of indicators and their weights, the range of procedures involved in collecting and analyzing data.
5. We refer the interested reader to relevant literature by the Grameen Foundation and ACCION, two of the groups that have developed tools to measure absolute poverty in relation to poverty lines. A summary of their work appears in an addendum to this chapter.
6. The wording of the legislation suggests that Congress intends for the *higher* of these two alternative criteria to provide the applicable extreme poverty line for a given country.
7. See Graham, forthcoming.

8. These additional eight countries are Albania, Ghana, Guatemala, India (Bihar and Uttar Pradesh only), Jamaica, Madagascar, Tajikistan, and Vietnam.

9. See http://www.povertytools.org/Project_Documents/Assessing%20and%20 Improving %20Accuracy.pdf for a more technical discussion of these accuracy measures. Note that the term "not very-poor" refers specifically to all clients who are not among the very poor (e.g., including those who are moderately poor, members of the middle class, and the rich) rather than being limited to those who, although poor, are not *very* poor..

10. Both errors are expressed as a percentage of the total number of very poor.

11. The *poverty incidence error* (PIE) criterion developed for this project is a relatively intuitive way to visualize the balance of errors. This criterion is equal to the difference between predicted poverty incidence and actual poverty incidence, expressed as a percentage. Due to the way the two concepts are defined, a zero-value PIE is equivalent to equalizing undercoverage and leakage, regardless of their size.

12. For details, see http://www.povertytools.org/Project_Documents/Assessing%20and%20 Improving%20Accuracy.pdf

13. While a number of valid questions have been raised about the capacity of the LSMS to act as a reliable benchmark, there is little debate about the fact that it is the least imperfect—and probably only available—instrument to play this role.

14. The questionnaires used in Bangladesh are available at www.povertytools.org.

15. There is considerable debate about the concept and value of international poverty lines and the computation of purchasing power parity rates (see, for example, Karshenas [2004] and Reddy and Pogge [2003]).

16. See Khandker's (2005) rigorous analysis on the impact of microfinance on poverty in Bangladesh.

17. These regression methods are ordinary least squares, quantile, linear probability, and probit. Most of them were also used in a two-step regression where the "not very-poor" are identified in a first step, after which the model with the best five, ten, or fifteen predictors is applied to the remaining part of the sample.

18. This is also the approach taken by ACCION and the Grameen Foundation (GF) as part of their internal efforts to measure the level of absolute poverty of their clients. GF has developed—or is in the process of developing—"Progress out of Poverty" indices for the Philippines, Mexico, India, Pakistan, Bangladesh, Bolivia, Haiti, Morocco, and Egypt (see Schreiner [2006] and http://www.gfusa.org). ACCION has worked on tools for Peru, Bolivia, Ecuador, El Salvador, and Haiti (see, e.g., Dewez et al. [2003] and Horn-Welch and Devaney [2002, 2003]). The ACCION tool is designed to directly measure expenditures rather than predicting them through the use of poverty indicators, which is the approach chosen by IRIS and GF. While both IRIS and GF use regression analysis to identify and select indicators, IRIS tested a larger number of regression techniques and implicitly included error balancing in its selection of the best-performing poverty indicators.

19. See http://www.povertytools.org/Field_Test/grantees.htm for a list of grantees and the countries in which they tested the practicality of USAID/IRIS draft tools.

20. Although USAID's mandate is that 50% of the agency's microenterprise funds reach the very poor, this requirement applies collectively to total funding and does not flow down to USAID's individual partners. In other words, no individual practitioner will be required to demonstrate that 50% of its clients are very poor. Despite repeated clarifications of this requirement, the impression remains among some practitioners that the 50% requirement applies to their clients and may affect their future funding, creating an incentive for strategic reporting of poverty outreach.

21. In addition, and as mentioned earlier in this chapter, only those tools that produce very low undercoverage and leakage errors can reliably be used for individual poverty scoring. To the extent that econometric techniques are used to select indicators and weights that balance errors over a sample of clients, individual scoring is as inadequate as it is unnecessary.

22. Other shortcut tools—such as Grameen Foundation's Progress out of Poverty Index or ACCION's poverty assessment tool—are similar in structure, length, and categories of indicators.

23. See Table 1 in Don Sillers's "National and International Poverty Lines: An Overview" for local-currency equivalents of $1/day in PPP terms for 90 countries. Available at http://www.povertytools.org/Project_Documents/Poverty_lines___An_Overview_1_ 4_06.pdf.

24. See   http://www.povertytools.org/Project_Documents/International_Tools_Note.pdf for a technical description of the development and testing of these international tools.

25. Information on the LSMS and the SDA survey are available at http://www-wds. worldbank.org/external/default/main?pagePK=64193027&piPK=64187937&the SitePK=523679&menuPK=64187510&searchMenuPK=64187511&theSitePK=52 3679&entityID=000178830_98101911083938&searchMenuPK=64187511&the SitePK=523679.

26. The current level of knowledge about indicator-based poverty assessment tools makes it challenging to confidently determine the ideal frequency of tool adjustment. In countries experiencing sustained economic growth, tools may need to be adjusted every three to five years. In countries where growth is slower, a lag of five to ten years may be acceptable. One strategy to reduce the number of adjustments is to select indicators that appear to be more robust over time in predicting poverty status, although this issue itself deserves further research.

27. The necessary sample size differs based on the level of precision required and the statistical properties of the impact indicators in the sample. These characteristics will vary from country to country—hence the difficulty in specifying a minimum sample size. As an indication, the sample size for the USAID/IRIS accuracy tests was 800 households.

28. This problem is further complicated by the fact that practitioner organizations as well as policymakers may differ in their assessment of how serious undercoverage is compared with leakage (i.e., is it worse to incorrectly classify a very poor household as not very-poor than to make the opposite error?). Some practitioners may not be particularly concerned if a tool incorrectly includes some nonpoor clients in the "very poor" group as long as it ensures that most of the very poor are correctly identified. Others may wish to focus their operations exclusively on the very poor and would therefore need targeting tools that have a lower leakage error even at the expense of a higher undercoverage error. In coordination with USAID, IRIS selected the neutral option, assuming that both errors were equally detrimental to meeting the objectives of the congressional mandate.

29. Note that measuring movement across poverty lines is a necessary but not sufficient condition for measuring impact. Any improvement in wealth among clients over time may just be a secular trend that is also observed in the nonclient population. Therefore, to measure impact, appropriate research designs and econometric techniques need to be used in combination with poverty assessment tools. This involves the sampling of a suitable control group (i.e., of nonclients) and the measurement of clients and nonclients over time, preferably using a panel study framework.

ADDENDUM: EXPERIENCE OF GRAMEEN FOUNDATION AND ACCION INTERNATIONAL

Nigel Biggar and Rekha Reddy

The following section describes two promising tools developed by Grameen Foundation and ACCION International, respectively. Although the tools use different approaches, they can both be used to measure absolute poverty in relation to poverty lines.

Grameen Foundation
Progress out of Poverty Index

Grameen Foundation (GF) has as its ultimate goal the elimination of absolute poverty in the shortest possible time frame. To this end, the organization has developed a tool called the Progress out of Poverty Index (PPI) to support the work of microfinance institutions (MFIs) in reaching and serving the poorest members of their communities. This tool accurately and cost-effectively assesses the likelihood that clients are poor and tracks movement across poverty thresholds. With this instrument, MFI managers can segment their portfolios based on the poverty levels of their clients and determine what products and services meet various clients' needs. This will enable MFIs to contribute to the achievement of the Millennium Development Goals of reducing extreme poverty. An example of the PPI (constructed for Mexico) is provided in Figure 1.2.

Progress out of Poverty Index

The PPI is a country-specific tool that is a composite of easy-to-collect, verifiable, nonfinancial indicators. These indicators are tailored to each country's particular economic situation and typically include family size, number of children attending school, type of housing, and what the family normally eats. Indicators are derived from national household surveys (for example, Mexico's ENIGH database or Pakistan's Integrated Household Survey) and are selected based on the degree to which they predict a household's poverty level. By using indicators from a national household survey that tracks income and expenditure, the PPI provides the most accurate estimate of the *probability* that a client is poor. Repeated application of the PPI permits MFIs to track client movement across poverty lines over time.

Figure 1.2 Mexico Progress out of Poverty Index: Ten Indicators

Indicator	Attributes					Points
1. Does the house have a shower?				No	Yes	
				0	5	
2. How many household members are from 0 to 17 years old?	Four or more	Three	Two	One	Zero	
	0	7	12	18	28	
3. Household has fixed line telephone or cellular?				No	Yes	
				0	7	
4. Household has a car, truck, small truck, etc.?				No	Yes	
				0	8	
5. How many household members are wage earning employees?			Zero	One	Two or more	
			0	2	7	
6. Highest grade of study of the female head of household/wife?			Up to 6th Grade of primary School	Up to 6th semester or 3rd year of Vocational School	7th semester of High School or more	
			0	4	16	
7. In the past month has the household purchased fabric softener?				No	Yes	
				0	5	
8. In the past three months has clothing been purchased for household members of 17 years of age or more?				No	Yes	
				0	6	
9. Of what material are the floors of the house constructed primarily?			Earth	Cement	Wood or Tile	
			0	7	11	
10. In the past week did any household member eat in a cafeteria, taco shop, etc.?				No	Yes	
				0	7	
					Total:	

Source: Calculations by Microfinance Risk Management L.L.C. based on ENIGH 2002

Measurement and Management

The PPI is both a measurement and a management tool. By measuring clients' poverty levels and how they change over time, MFIs can segment their portfolios to focus on client recruitment, repayment, and retention by poverty band to determine how well their products and services meet client needs.

By using the PPI, MFIs should be able to

- Systematically document changes in client poverty status to verify mission adherence and achievement

- Target products and services by dividing clients into distinct poverty bands (very poor, moderately poor, and nonpoor) and track results by poverty band across different performance indicators (recruitment, repayment, exit, default, etc.)

- Better meet clients' needs through the development of increasingly client-focused products and delivery systems, which also should lead to improvements in the MFI's levels of competitiveness, profitability, and client retention

- Provide timely and accurate information to socially responsible investors and other key stakeholders

Practical and Reliable

Any poverty measurement tool must be both practical and reliable. This is critical if MFIs are to integrate it into operations and manage their institutions according to the information it generates.

In integrating the PPI into operations, MFI staff determine what data collection methods work best in their field operations. In many cases, loan officers already collect a lot of information as part of their routine client assessment work. Initial field testing of the PPI has shown that loan officers can streamline this data collection and save time by asking fewer questions (the PPI typically has only ten indicators). The use of indicators that are simple to collect, easy to verify, and difficult to manipulate helps to ensure that the data generated by the PPI are reliable. GF is working with its network partners to support the integration of PPI data into their Management Information Systems (MIS) so they can generate timely and accurate reports on client performance across poverty bands.

Collaborative Effort

GF is building PPIs for all markets where its partners operate. In the next twelve months PPIs will be available for India, Pakistan, Bangladesh, the

Philippines, Mexico, Haiti, Bolivia, Morocco, and Egypt. Once a PPI is built for a market, it is a public good made available to all who wish to use it. GFUSA will continue to collaborate with other key stakeholders in the microfinance industry to ensure that the PPI is available to the greatest possible number of MFIs that wish to better meet the needs of the poorest members of the communities they serve.

To learn more about the Progress out of Poverty Index and GF's Social Performance Management initiatives, contact the GF Washington, DC, office at (202) 628-3560 or go to www.gfusa.org.

ACCION International's Poverty Assessment Tool[1]

In 2002 ACCION began its poverty assessment project in an effort to understand and measure the poverty levels of the microfinance clients of its affiliates. ACCION sought to capture information on client households and businesses in a readily usable form to measure MFI outreach to the poor. These findings on poverty would then be incorporated into a regular reporting system enabling institutions to monitor outreach regularly and to develop or amend products and strategies to reach clients of a lower socioeconomic status.

ACCION designed its poverty assessment tool to address the following questions:

- How does the poverty distribution of the clients of ACCION's affiliates compare with the poverty distribution of the country's overall population? How do these clients compare with national and international poverty lines?

- How do the demographic and socioeconomic characteristics (such as gender, household size, education, and housing) of the clients of ACCION's affiliates compare with the overall population, and how are these characteristics correlated with poverty?

- What are the general borrowing patterns of poorer clients? How are loan size, repayment amount, loan maturity, number of previous loans, and repayment status related to poverty level?

- What sources of data can provide this information most readily and reliably? In particular, what are the pros and cons of using client loan evaluation data and/or household survey data?

Methodology and Data

The first phase of ACCION's poverty assessment project was characterized by the following three premises:

1. ACCION chose a "standard of living" approach to measure poverty by collecting data on income and expenditure, rather than using proxy indicators.

2. ACCION began by using data collected as part of the routine credit evaluation process that were available in the management information system (MIS) databases of the institutions. Using such data in poverty monitoring and assessment was desirable because its collection is automatic and entails no additional cost to an institution's operations.

3. ACCION sought to develop an "absolute" measure of poverty, defined by actual levels of income and expenditure, rather than a relative measure, in which clients are ranked among a group of people. With a relative measure, all that can be said is whether one person is better off than another, even though both could be poor or nonpoor. Only an absolute measure would allow comparisons with the national and international poverty studies used to determine poverty lines and track national poverty distributions. After pursuing these premises, we remained focused on the standard-of-living approach, and have determined that loan evaluation data from the institutions' MIS databases can be a practical, low-cost source of information for monitoring poverty levels on a regular basis.

ACCION made use of the following three data sources:

- Loan evaluation data collected by MFI affiliates through the credit evaluation process.

- Publicly available data from national household surveys such as the World Bank's Living Standards Measurement Study (LSMS). These data tracked nonclients and were used to compare the poverty level of clients with that of nonclients in the region or country.

- Household surveys that focused on income and expenditure. Modeled after the LSMS, ACCION conducted these surveys to compare clients' poverty levels against national poverty lines and to assess the comparability of MFI data with national survey data.

Absolute Measures of Poverty

To determine whether MIS data could be used to measure absolute poverty levels with reference to national norms, ACCION compared data collected through an LSMS-type household survey with data from the same client households collected through the institution's own credit evaluation process.

After a poverty distribution was determined, a range of analyses of client behavior became possible. ACCION proposed a model for regular reporting called the social scorecard. The social scorecard is a poverty outreach report that disaggregates commonly used indicators by level of relative poverty, as shown in Table 1.6. Level 1 represents clients who are below the poverty line, and level 2 includes the group of vulnerable nonpoor clients (with earnings of 100–150% of the poverty line amount).

The social scorecard can also be modified as requested by an MFI to report poverty data by geographic region or product type. All the institutions should incorporate this social scorecard as a regular report in their MIS. It should be one of the reports monitored regularly as part of overall performance monitoring along with financial indicators. The social scorecard is thus intended to be part of the data that management regularly presents to the board of the institution; eventually, management is expected to be able to set targets for the levels of these indicators in strategic and business planning exercises.

Table 1.6   Abbreviated Model of a Social Scorecard

Statistics by Poverty Level	Percentage of Clients	Percentage of Loan Portfolio	Percentage of New Clients	Average Household Income	Average Loan Size and Balance	Percentage of Portfolio at Risk	Percentage of Clients with Savings
Level 1: poor clients	54.6	50.3	57.5	2,606	3,411	3.5	20.2
Level 2: vulnerable nonpoor clients	16.1	16.7	16.0	3,527	3,928	2.9	25.5
Level 3: nonpoor clients	29.3	33.0	26.5	4,582	4,235	3.0	30.7

Source: ACCION model based on a microfinance institution database sample.

Management Use of Poverty Measurement Tool

The institutions we work with have already been motivated to make changes in their operations as a result of the poverty assessment process. Mibanco, for example, views poverty reporting as a way for the institution to understand and move into an untapped market of poorer clients, particularly those in rural areas. BancoSol has expressed interest in integrating information from the social scorecard into its Balanced Scorecard. Sogesol used information on the comparisons between household survey data and loan evaluation data to guide their loan officers in gathering better data for the credit evaluation. Before the poverty study, credit evaluations gathered income and expenditure data for the potential client for a particular month and often did not pick up important expenses that are paid annually in Haiti, such as school fees and rent. Now Sogesol loan officers are instructed to look beyond daily expenses and seek information on these less common categories of expense. If expenses are below a certain percentage of income on the credit evaluation, loan officers need to seek special approval from an official on the credit committee.

Poverty analysis can also be used indirectly to improve data collection procedures. During a recent ACCION working group meeting, attendees discussed the possibility of changing loan evaluation forms to get a more accurate representation of household size after learning about discrepancies in household size information gathered through the ACCION household survey and MFI client forms.

Assessing the Accuracy of the Social Scorecard

Using the expenditure data from the more detailed household survey as a benchmark, we sought to estimate how accurate the social scorecard was in classifying the clients into the "correct" poverty level. Table 1.7 shows the level of overlap between the poverty levels obtained from the two data sources. Results were similar for BancoSol and Mibanco. Approximately 45% of the microfinance clients in the samples of these three institutions were categorized in the same poverty level for the household survey data and the loan evaluation data. Approximately 35% of clients were categorized in poverty levels that differed by one level for the household survey data and the loan evaluation data. Approximately 20% of clients differed by more than one poverty level between the two sets of data.

Analysis of income tells a similar story. The higher accuracy of the Sogesol scorecard highlights an important issue: the percentage of clients correctly classified is directly related to the overall incidence of poverty. Since approximately half of the clients in the sample are sorted into the correct poverty

Table 1.7   Comparison of Poverty Levels Obtained through the Household Survey and the Social Scorecard

Expenditure per Capita	BancoSol, Bolivia	Mibanco, Peru	Sogesol, Haiti
Same poverty level	45%	46%	60%
Difference of one poverty level	32%	39%	18%
Difference of two poverty levels	23%	15%	22%

Source: MFI loan data and ACCION household survey data.

level, we conclude that using credit evaluation data in a social scorecard format provides these MFIs with a practical, low-cost tool to regularly monitor the poverty level of clients.

Plans for Future Research

ACCION chose the standard-of-living approach to poverty assessment to take advantage of household financial data collected in the loan evaluations of the institutions studied. The next challenge, however, is to define and implement a methodology for institutions that do not collect detailed household financial data for their clients or do not record these data in a sound and reliable database.

A second challenge is to incorporate the social scorecard into the regular processes of performance monitoring and strategic planning for additional institutions.

To learn more about the Poverty Assessment Project, contact ACCION at (202) 393-5113 or visit www.accion.org/pubs.

Notes

30. This section is an excerpt from SEEP Network Progress Note No. 10, October 2005. For more information on the Progress Note series, visit www.seepnetwork.org.
31. For more details, refer to ACCION InSights #1, #5, #8, and #13, which detail the framework for ACCION's poverty tool and the findings of poverty assessments for Mibanco in Peru, Sogesol in Haiti, and BancoSol in Bolivia. These free publications are available for download at http://www.accion.org/insight/.
32. National poverty lines come from a variety of sources, the most common of which are governments and national household surveys, such as the World Bank's LSMS or those performed by the United Nations or the Inter-American Development Bank's Program for the Improvement of Surveys and the Measurement of Living Conditions in Latin America and the Caribbean (MECOVI) in partnership with national statistical institutes.

2

Factors That Contribute to Exponential Growth: Case Studies for Massive Outreach to the Poor and Poorest

Alex Counts, Roshaneh Zafar, and Erin Connor

INTRODUCTION

The argument for accelerated growth in microfinance is based on the persistence of mass poverty and the fact that microfinance has proven to be one of the few antipoverty approaches that is both effective and scalable. However, barriers to microfinance outreach remain and must be overcome if optimal levels are to be attained.

Rapid growth (in terms of client outreach) should be pursued aggressively and with a sense of urgency wherever growth-ready microfinance institutions (MFIs) are operating in a reasonably enabling environment. Backing aggressive expansion plans of well-prepared MFIs impacts those clients that are reached and can also have a significant impact by demonstrating the growth potential of the overall sector while spurring innovation. Exponential growth can also enable MFIs to realize economies of scale, allowing for the lowering of interest rates.

Factors Contributing to Rapid Growth

Based on the trailblazing experiences of Grameen Bank and other MFIs in Bangladesh, as well as the three case studies highlighted in this chapter, the most important factors contributing to the success of rapid MFI expansion can be summarized as follows:

- *Strong entrepreneurial leadership.* Although effective leadership can take many forms, it is essential to assure financiers, regulators, staff, board, and clients that the sacrifices required for rapid growth are worthwhile and will result in success.

- *Adequate financing.* Ongoing liquidity and funding are absolutely essential for scaling microfinance institutions; even a temporary liquidity crisis can cripple an otherwise sound expansion strategy.

- *Some degree of regulatory support.* Among the activities that scaling MFIs need to be effectively permitted to undertake by the government are lending to the poor for productive activities; receiving external financing or being able to mobilize deposits; hiring and compensating employees; and charging interest rates compatible with long-range sustainability in the particular market.

- *Strong focus on microfinance, sustainability, and effectively serving a particular niche.* MFIs should focus primarily on providing microfinance to the poor, with other services being secondary and consistent with the goal of sustainable growth of the MFI and its clients' businesses. However, well-designed "credit plus" programs can be essential in ensuring that income gains of clients are sustained, which in turn ensures the long-run viability of the MFI.

- *A large unserved market.* For obvious reasons, relatively large numbers of poor people who do not have access to microfinance services are needed in order for any growth strategy to succeed.

- *Ability to attract, harness, and retain talent at all levels.* MFIs must be able to recruit, develop, and keep quality employees in order to sustain growth. Performance-based incentives (financial and nonfinancial) and promotion as well as training opportunities are often important elements of strategies to achieve this.

- *Effective information management systems and financial controls.* Having a system that produces relatively accurate and timely information becomes especially critical as an organization reaches scale, as it allows for effective decision making and prevention of fraud.

Some of the nonessential but important factors that can contribute to the success of a growth strategy are a strong core team beyond the CEO, good governance and strong stakeholder support, financial products that respond to a clear need among the target population, and country-wide economic and monetary stability.

This chapter features three institutions: Fondation Zakoura in Morocco, Kashf Foundation in Pakistan, and Amhara Credit and Savings Institution in Ethiopia. Through these case studies we will address in greater depth the conditions necessary to allow for exponential growth.

Fondation Zakoura: Morocco

Fondation Zakoura, based in Casablanca, Morocco, experienced its period of greatest growth from January 2000 to December 2002, during which time it grew from 16,055 to 103,720 clients. During this period, Zakoura's client outreach grew at an average annual rate of 87%, and its loan portfolio increased from $1.53 million to $15.9 million. The operating expense ratio declined by more than one-third, from 27.59% to 17.12%. Portfolio at risk (PAR) remained below 1% throughout. As of March 2006, Zakoura had reached a total of 193,787 clients.

Key factors that contributed to Zakoura's growth during the period under study include its confident, risk-taking leadership; a supportive regulatory framework; and Zakoura's early willingness to take on local currency debt. A grant of $3.7 million from the Hassan II Fund came at a critical time, and cost control at every level of the organization ensured that it was used prudently. Zakoura's effectiveness at securing resources and designing systems "on the fly" as it scaled up was critical, and its alliance with Save the Children was also important.

Kashf Foundation: Pakistan

Kashf Foundation, founded in 1997 and based in Lahore, Pakistan, underwent a period of exponential growth from 2001 to 2003. During this two-year period, Kashf's client outreach grew from approximately 7,000 to over 45,000 clients, for a growth rate of 117% from 2001 to 2002 and 189% between 2002 and 2003. Throughout this entire period, PAR remained below 2%. As of March 2006, Kashf had reached a total of 80,191 clients.

The most critical factors contributing to Kashf's growth during this period include a clear organizational vision, strong leadership, sound corporate governance, and a singular focus on financial service delivery to the poor. A period of preparation prior to the growth period was used to adjust the methodology, standardize products and systems, and develop simple and easily replicable products. By charging a price for its services that would make the program sustainable within five years, Kashf was able to grow with reduced dependence on grants (compared with other

MFIs in Pakistan) and to avoid the need to raise interest rates later. However, the availability of grants and low-interest loans during its growth period was essential, as they ensured adequate liquidity and sufficient resources to build the infrastructure and internal capacity needed for rapid growth.

Amhara Credit and Savings Institution (ACSI): Ethiopia

Over the span of four years (2001–2005), ACSI nearly tripled in size, from 150,000 clients to more than 434,000. During this time, ACSI maintained a repayment rate of 99% and an operating expense ratio under 10%. This regulated MFI showed that even in challenging regions of sub-Saharan Africa rapid growth and cost containment are achievable. As of April 2006, ACSI had reached a total of 446,625 clients.

Upon careful review, the essential factors contributing to ACSI's growth were an overwhelming demand in an underserved market; strong support for the growth among all levels of staff; and regulatory support through Ethiopia's microfinance law, which was enacted in 1994. ACSI's ability to collect savings and on-lend these funds has been a key factor in its ability to ensure liquidity (the MFI had mobilized almost US$29 million in net savings as of December 2005). Strategic and consistent donor support was also especially beneficial to ACSI in the first few years of its growth phase. The support of the local government has been helpful in many respects but challenging in others. A credit delivery methodology based on group lending and risk assessment by respected local people has served it well, but with increasing competition it may need to be revised in the coming years. In addition, an enlightened approach to human resource development has been important, along with the strong leadership of ACSI's executive director.

Bearing the lessons from these and other successful growth experiences in mind, and the vast numbers of poor families worldwide who have not been reached, a sustained global effort to scale up microfinance for the poor and poorest is clearly needed and would represent a sound investment toward reaching the Millennium Development Goals. Microfinance managers and boards, regulators, financial institutions, donor agencies, the media, researchers, and the general public all have critical roles to play in this effort.

THE CASE FOR URGENT AND STRATEGIC PROMOTION OF EXPONENTIAL GROWTH

The core argument for promoting the rapid growth of microfinance for the poor, and especially for the poorest,[1] can be summarized by recounting two scandals of our time. The first is the persistence of extreme poverty in a world of plenty, with no massive global effort to reduce it. The second scandal is the astonishing underinvestment of financial, human, and intellectual capital in the refinement and growth of one of the few antipoverty approaches that can grow to become financially self-sustaining.[2] While there are many ways to approach poverty alleviation, microfinance is exceptional if not unique in that it combines a robust antipoverty strategy with strong business discipline that enables it to self-finance to a large extent. In other words, rather than representing a trade-off, scale and sustainability can go hand in hand and, in fact, reinforce each other. Still, the inability of most MFIs to achieve optimal scale continues to stymie microfinance's contribution to the reduction of global poverty. This chapter will attempt to demystify this process of rapid scaling by studying three organizations that have achieved strong growth, which, if replicated by the hundreds of other growth-ready MFIs, could play a major role in achieving the Microcredit Summit and Millennium Development Goals. The opportunity was summed up well by microfinance practitioner, donor, and advocate Marshall Saunders, who said, "In this world of plenty, poverty continues to be with us as it always has. However, the ability to scale up microcredit to millions of poor people in a sustainable way is new, and *known* to be effective. Yet, there is not a serious global effort to scale up. It's like smallpox, where the ability to prevent the disease was known two hundred years before its eradication."

Poverty is prevalent in scores of countries and afflicts approximately 3 billion people.[3] Particularly among the poorest one-third of this demographic, the costs in terms of wasted human potential, unnecessary suffering, civil unrest, and environmental degradation are staggering. Furthermore, poverty continues to have a predominantly female face; 70% of the world's poorest are women.[4] The link between the scaling of microfinance, the reduction of poverty, and the empowerment of women is best seen in the case of Bangladesh, where microfinance not only has contributed to lower poverty rates (which have been documented elsewhere) but has also positively impacted the choice of family size and the education of female children. According to a recent study on demographic change by the International Centre for Diarrhoeal Disease Research in Bangladesh (ICCRD,B), the fertility rate in Bangladesh has decreased from 7 children in the 1970s to 3.3 by 2000. This drastic decline in fertility can be attributed to changes in income levels, women's education, age at marriage, and women's empowerment; according to several studies, microfinance has positively influenced several of these factors, including income, access to resources, women's empowerment, and even the ability to pay for girls' education. Despite this, microfinance has been comprehensively scaled up only in a very small number of countries, such as Bangladesh and Bolivia, even though it has been shown to work effectively in most nations where poverty persists. Many growth-ready MFIs have seen their business plans languish and their capacity to grow remain untapped.

It is important to review some of the arguments for pursuing modest growth, as they have some merit. Clearly, not every MFI is prepared for rapid growth—which, for the purposes of this chapter, is defined as annual growth in outreach of 65% or more for at least two years—at every phase of its existence. Some are never prepared for such an effort. Pursuing rapid growth without adequate preparation can lead to organizational stress and even meltdown, which could constitute a setback for the entire microfinance sector in a country or region and require decades of "re-educating" clients on the mores of credit discipline. Pursuing slower growth by financing expansion largely from the retained earnings of profitable institutions, rather than from external sources of finance as is usually required during a time of rapid expansion, may place less of a strain on the human and financial resources of MFIs.

However, a central tenet of this chapter is that rapid growth should be pursued aggressively and with a sense of urgency wherever certain preconditions are met, the most basic being the existence of MFIs that can demonstrate the potential and commitment to achieve strong growth and poverty reduction. The case for promotion of rapid growth can be summarized in the following five arguments:

1. Maximum Poverty Reduction

With the growing evidence that microfinance contributes to the reduction of poverty, including extreme poverty,[5] it stands to reason that where the preconditions for rapid growth are in place, and where poverty is rampant, a serious effort should be made to support all "growth-ready" MFIs in making the maximum contribution to the achievement of national and international poverty reduction goals. A detailed study by Khandker (2005) of panel data from Bangladesh reveals that microfinance has a considerable impact on reducing poverty, particularly among women, along with enhancing economic opportunities for the village or community as a whole. Khandker has also shown that the MFIs targeting the poorest (those below $1/day per capita) are comparable in financial performance to those MFIs not reaching the poorest. In other words, scale, sustainability, poverty targeting, and impact can go hand in hand.

Identifying growth-ready MFIs is critical in the context of resource-constrained environments, as it can lead to better results and less waste of critical resources. It is important to remember that growth is not an end in itself but a means to achieving larger goals of poverty reduction. If an MFI appears to be failing in its goal of reducing poverty (either by not reaching the poor or not benefiting them), the development case for scaling it is questionable—notwithstanding any potential to generate profits or increase client outreach through instituting a growth strategy. Several impact studies have shown that microfinance acts as an income-smoothing opportunity for households, along with enhancing incomes in the long run.

2. The Demonstration Effect

When at least one MFI has the courage and support necessary for rapid growth, and succeeds in doing so, this often has the effect of prompting others to grow, essentially representing a "public good." This dynamic, once set in motion, can lead to sector-wide growth and innovation, as well as stimulating competition that benefits clients. This can be a self-reinforcing, virtuous cycle, but one that often needs a catalytic agent—a fast-growing MFI—to get the process started. Furthermore, it can prompt other corporate- and social-sector actors to think creatively about delivering nonfinancial services to the poor and poorest, either by piggybacking on the infrastructure of the larger MFI or simply by adapting the MFI's success strategy for creating financial and "social" profit where none was thought to exist before. Even where microfinance is relatively widespread, rapid growth in serving new niches (for example, the rural poor, the destitute, or beggars) or delivering new products (for example, micro-insurance or health education) can have the same demonstration effect but in a narrower sense. However, one word of caution here: is that big is not necessarily always better, especially if an MFI grows quickly by accessing subsidized funds and effectively passes those subsidies on to clients by charging interest rates that are clearly unsustainable. This is particularly true of some new microfinance banks that have been backed by governments, where the bottom line is measured in terms of numbers of clients rather than financial health. In such a case, a rapidly growing organization could stunt sectoral growth, at least in the medium term, even as the MFI itself grows.

3. Promotion of Learning and Innovation

While the promotion of rapid growth—which must be the top priority of an MFI's senior management to be successful—can temporarily stifle innovation in areas such as new product development and sector-wide collaborative work, it can also prompt breakthrough thinking and action. Types of innovation that have been achieved in times of rapid institutional growth include realizing and taking advantage of economies of scale; effective delegation and empowerment of mid-level staff (by necessity if not by design); recruitment and retention of staff (through rapid promotion of high performers); securing enhanced stakeholder participation and support; systematizing, standardizing, and simplifying policies and procedures; and crisis management. These growth-induced lessons are available to the MFI even after it slows its growth, and they might filter out to other MFIs who are likely studying the growth process. Those MFIs that proactively share their knowledge and experiences with others will experience enhanced and accelerated sector-wide impact.

4. Realizing Economies of Scale

Most MFIs are not optimally scaled and as a result are relatively inefficient. Due in part to the underinvestment in microfinance by development agencies, and the short time horizon for realizing profits of some commercial and quasi-commercial investors, the poor have been forced to pay for most of these inefficiencies through high interest rates and other fees. That the poor have been able to shoulder this burden reflects how productive and motivated they are, and demonstrates the long-term potential of microfinance as MFIs become more efficient. The high costs of MFIs can have significant development (poverty reduction) as well as political consequences. On the development side, if the estimate of $4 billion in outstanding micro-loans is correct, a reduction in effective annual interest rates of 5% (from, say, 25% to 20% on average) would mean an annual windfall of $200 million for the poor and could also reduce pressure from governments to impose restrictive and harmful interest rate caps. To put this in perspective, $200 million represents the equivalent of USAID's entire annual expenditure on microenterprise development. The recent reduction of interest rates by SHARE in India (from 30% to 20% effective) and Al Amana in Morocco (from 40% to 26% effective), due in part to realization of economies of scale, shows the potential for operating efficiencies to be passed along to the customer. At the first annual Sanabel conference in 2003, Beth Rhyne of ACCION presented an important study of the microfinance sector in Latin America that suggested similar long-term trends. Of course, it takes quality managers to realize economies of scale and to put the liberated resources to work for clients as well as the institution. While mergers and acquisitions may play a role in the realization of these cost reductions in some markets, the rapid expansion of MFIs to optimal scale must be a central part of this process. Another important consideration is the extent to which quality MFIs have to externalize equity investments. In most cases where these investments are readily available, it becomes easier to pass on cost reductions to clients since retained earnings need not be the main contributor to building the equity base required for growth. In particular, these retained earnings need not be used for leveraging commercial debt or for absorbing the short-term losses of branches before they break even.

5. Influencing Regulators and Policymakers

While it is clear that some minimal degree of effective regulatory support for microfinance is a precondition for rapid growth, MFIs have expanded quickly under regulatory regimes that were far from optimal.[6] Often, the experience and achievements of MFIs that have somehow managed to grow rapidly have been essential advocacy tools in convincing regulators to be more supportive of microfinance and micro-entrepreneurs—shattering the "Catch-22" where growth is impossible without regulatory support, but regulatory support cannot be secured until growth and widespread impact are shown to be possible. While this can be risky for the pioneering MFI serving as the "guinea pig" to prove that growth is possible even under suboptimal conditions, it can have major benefits for the entire sector. The ripple effect can extend beyond national borders. For example, according to Jamal Dadi of USAID Morocco, the presentations on the achievements of the microfinance sectors in Bangladesh, Bolivia, and Indonesia at the original Microcredit Summit in 1997 strongly influenced the Moroccan government to adopt a series of pro-microfinance policies that helped lead to rapid growth there (a growth experience that will be explored in some depth below). They did this despite the fact that there had not yet been a clear example of breakthrough expansion within Morocco. For these reasons, MFIs that have a credible plan for rapid growth should be supported because of the potential benefits for the sector at the national, regional, and even international levels.

While policy advocacy on regulatory matters affecting microfinance is often well intentioned, there are pitfalls to be avoided in such advocacy efforts. For example, some have advocated for regulatory policies in microfinance that, while appearing to have benefits for today's microfinance sector, are likely to limit future innovation and growth. Most often these policy shortcomings are seen in regulatory regimes that too narrowly define the products offered, clients served, or even institutional forms approved for the delivery of microfinance services.

THE BANGLADESH EXPERIENCE

The achievements of today's microfinance sector required the demonstration that the provision of financial services to the poor and especially the poorest could be done in a replicable and profitable manner on a national scale through private-sector institutions. There is little doubt that the Grameen Bank served as a global trailblazer, closely followed by BRAC, ASA, and in due course many other Bangladeshi MFIs. As a result, today the outreach of the microfinance sector in this country is an astonishing 15 million families, or more than 55% of the entire population of the country (and a larger percentage of the poor and poorest, since most programs, including the large ones that operate primarily in rural areas, are means tested).

Grameen Bank and the many other high-quality MFIs varying in size and approach that today serve the poor of Bangladesh had some unique advantages, including effective (though not explicit) regulatory support and relatively large amounts of development capital available for well-performing institutions with entrepreneurial leaders. We also believe that one of the key reasons for Grameen's success was the impressive capacity of Professor Muhammad Yunus and other Bangladeshi microfinance leaders to empower the people who worked with them and to provide them with a vision that they could believe in. The density and homogeneity of the population certainly helped, as did the fact that despite frequent *hartals* (general strikes) that negatively affected the cities and foreign investment, the rural areas were spared to some degree, and the situation never boiled over to civil war. However, there were significant and to some extent unique obstacles that were overcome in realizing this breakthrough that provide lessons for future growth in the sector, and for that reason they are explored briefly below.

When no set of microfinance best practices and performance benchmarks exists, as was the case when the scaling up in Bangladesh began, the only option is to create them through trial and error even amid rapid growth. Initially, donors prevented Bangladeshi MFIs from using savings for on-lending, even though today this is seen as a best practice. There was widespread access to subsidized credit (mostly from so-called nationalized commercial banks) among the middle and upper classes, which often functioned as political patronage and could often be defaulted on with impunity, making enforcement of credit discipline among the poor challenging. Special legislation had to be written and a wholesale funding institution (PKSF) established to facilitate the growth and proliferation of MFIs—something the early leaders strongly supported even though it hastened the rise of competitors. Major natural disasters struck in 1981, 1987, 1988, 1991, 1995 and 1998—throwing many leading MFIs and their clients backward, at least temporarily—and had to be overcome. Finally, there were batteries of donor missions and unofficial delegations from virtually every country in the world who wanted to study this emerging success, all of whom were received graciously despite the hundreds of thousands of person-days required to do so. Many of those who visited went on to become microfinance pioneers in their own countries.[7]

Having achieved scale, the Bangladeshi microfinance sector is now leapfrogging ahead with a new cycle of innovation in areas such as serving the destitute, using microfinance as a broad platform for social change through multiple companies, savings mobilization, and development of client-friendly products. Since the story of this success has been told many times, it is not a major focus of this chapter; however, the achievements of the MFIs that are detailed in the following sections, and indeed the entire experience of rapid growth globally, would be impossible if it were not for the early and continuing leadership in Bangladesh.

FACTORS CONTRIBUTING TO EXPONENTIAL GROWTH

Based on our own experiences and interviews with dozens of thought and practice leaders to identify the key factors that contribute to successful rapid growth, we developed two lists: those factors that can arguably be termed "essential" and those that can play an important role. Both types of factors are summarized below.

1. Strong entrepreneurial leadership. This quality cannot be overemphasized. Effective leadership can take many forms and is essential to assuring and inspiring financiers (donors/investors/lenders), regulators, staff, board, and clients that the sacrifices required for rapid growth are worthwhile and will result in success. There can be no doubt that the leader will see the process through and is prepared to stay as long as necessary to reap the rewards and deal with the negative repercussions of growth. A singular dedication and commitment to advancing the long-term welfare of the target customer—the poor micro-entrepreneur—is critical, particularly if growth is seen not as a goal in and of itself, but as a means to achieving the reduction of poverty, including extreme poverty. In the words of one microfinance practitioner, "The top management must eat, breathe, sleep, and be microfinance." However, this is not necessarily a sufficient or even the most important quality of a leader who can manage rapid growth. In the words of another respected microfinance professional, "I think that there are important attributes of leaders that may be more important to success than being immersed in microfinance. I have seen very committed microfinance managers who eat, sleep, and breathe microfinance but are absolutely hopeless in spurring innovation, offering strong leadership, spotting entrepreneurial opportunities, or empowering staff." Success in growing an MFI exponentially requires special but by no means unique individuals.

2. **Adequate financing.** While it is not absolutely necessary to have financing lined up for the entire growth plan, as it was not for any of the case studies discussed in this chapter, ongoing sources of liquidity and funding are clearly needed for scaling microfinance institutions. Otherwise, the microfinance institution is likely to engage in destructive start/stop cycles that can significantly undermine the institution's credibility with its stakeholders and customers and hence impede the achievement of rapid growth. In Professor Yunus's words, "When there is not enough funding, you don't take big steps: you don't know if you'll fall off a cliff or if you'll continue to take steps."

In addition to securing adequate liquidity, the back-office functions of microfinance institutions need to be upgraded to ensure adequate asset/liability and cash flow management. Of course, such management is possible only if senior staff have developed realistic budgets, which include, among other things, adequate allocations for information systems and human resources. Microfinance managers also need the skills and instincts required to close critical deals on favorable terms with philanthropic and/or commercial financiers, and the self-confidence and mission orientation to turn down alliances that do not make sense. Scarce subsidies must be intelligently used to build the capacity of the institution to scale up, and not be treated as an out-and-out subsidy passed on to clients.

3. **Some degree of regulatory support.** Growth is very unlikely to succeed if at least one arm of the government does not effectively give its blessing to the existence and growth of microfinance. Among the activities that scaling MFIs must effectively be permitted to undertake are lending to the poor for productive activities, receiving external financing (or being able to mobilize deposits and having appropriate legal authority to on-lend those funds), hiring and compensating employees, and charging interest rates that are compatible with long-range sustainability in that market. Our view is that bank prudential regulation and supervision become necessary when MFIs start

mobilizing deposits from the public or when microfinance activities pose systemic risks to the financial sector, and not before that. Bangladesh is something of an anomaly in that the bank regulators chose to remain silent about the fact that many MFIs were raising deposits for on-lending. Despite that, there have been very few reported failures of MFIs in the Bangladeshi market, which says a great deal about the important role that leadership played in establishing sound and credible financial standards. However, this is not necessarily a prudent model to be followed. For example, several cases have been reported in Kenya of MFIs being set up to mobilize deposits on fraudulent lines, and that had to be closed down by the Central Bank.

4. Strong focus on (a) microfinance, (b) sustainability, and (c) effectively serving a particular niche. MFIs and their leaders need to be focused primarily if not exclusively on providing financial services to the poor, with other services (if provided) being secondary and subject to possible phasing out if they are not consistent with sustainable growth of the MFI and its clients' businesses. Of course, adding depth to these financial services and well-designed nonfinancial services is critical in order for an MFI to develop over time. As their market matures, the MFIs will face the need to diversify into other services such as micro-insurance or remittances. It is important to note, though, that a growth phase may not be the ideal time to bring in new product lines. MFIs that are part of larger, multisectoral NGOs are very unlikely to achieve rapid growth, which is rarely workable when the same field staff have to run subsidized programs along with microfinance activities. This suggests that the microfinance arms of such organizations be spun off as independent institutions prior to any sustained growth effort. (However, nonfinancial services integrated into microfinance can be a powerful part of an MFI's value proposition to clients and can represent a competitive advantage, although we believe it is best to have them in place before rapid growth commences.) MFIs also need to be at or close to operational sustainability, with a plan that will maintain if not enhance profitability over time. Finally, MFIs need to be clear about the target group they are serving and critically review opportunities to serve other groups that may have different needs, and which may be best avoided even if funding is available to do so. One of the authors recalls spending time in a village served by Grameen Bank and hearing from field staff that a localized repayment problem (later solved) was the result of the recruitment of non-poor clients to meet an outreach goal. Since these clients had different needs and motivations that were not compatible with Grameen's products and delivery style, they were not well served, and many did not repay their loans. This is not to say that serving the less poor is something to be avoided in general. Presumably, the somewhat better-off clients were not served by other MFIs or banks and needed microfinance to improve their standard of living. Yet it is our contention that being overly opportunistic and taking on nontraditional clients can have negative repercussions, particularly in a growth phase. There are other problems that can result from integrating nontraditional clients without adequate preparation, such as a high rate of client attrition that can hinder sustainability plans and retard growth. There is also a great deal of space to improve and establish customer care practices within microfinance in order to improve the well-being and satisfaction of clients.

5. A large unserved market. If the market that an MFI wishes to serve is not large, or is already well served by other providers who have similar products, then rapid growth is unlikely to succeed. On the other hand, a large market that is poorly served or unserved sets the stage for rapid growth if other conditions are met. Very small countries or ones with a small percentage of people in poverty are unlikely to attract the financial and human capital required for rapid growth. Countries with a large but very dispersed population present challenges in this context as well. While these challenges are not necessarily insurmountable, they may require relaxing the definition of rapid growth.

6. Ability to attract, harness, and retain talent at all levels. MFIs need to be able to recruit, develop, and keep quality employees in order to sustain growth. In some markets, such as those in South Asia, there is a nearly limitless pool of educated, unemployed men and (to a lesser degree) women who can serve as loan officers and branch managers. The challenge there lies primarily in training entry-level employees to take on greater responsibilities, particularly if filling middle-level and senior positions from within the organization is a goal, as we believe it should be. This building of a cadre of promotion-worthy entry-level staff is critical, since it is our view that the South Asian microfinance sector may suffer a crisis in terms of middle-tier managers during the next five years, which is compounded if one is committed to creating a gender balance within an organization. Throughout the global microfinance community, a plan for developing and supporting senior managers is crucial for achieving and sustaining growth. This is a key responsibility of the CEO, and if he or she does not embrace it and prove reasonably equal to it, growth is likely to be stunted or unsustainable. Furthermore, the governance structures of scaling microfinance institutions must evolve to respond to the risks and stresses inherent in pursuing a rapid growth strategy. For example, the board of directors should create an environment conducive to retaining a quality CEO and to putting a succession plan in place.

7. Effective information management systems and financial controls. Exponential growth requires increased delegation, and for that to work some system that allows reasonably accurate information to flow throughout the organization in a timely manner is essential. As has been documented by the

Grameen Technology Center and others, information systems ideally should be automated and have adequate support from the vendor who developed the product ("home-grown" systems have a very poor track record). But these information systems may be manual or hybrids if they can serve the purpose during the growth period.[8] Not only must they provide information, but that information must be effectively used by key decision makers. Microfinance expert Deborah Burand notes, "What we are talking about is not only hardware and software but also about management that knows how to harness and use technology. It is this latter point—management technology expertise—that often limits an MFI's ability to use technology to scale." The risks of not having adequate systems include fraud, deterioration of the portfolio, and negative impacts on clients; reasonably good systems allow for timely corrective action when problems such as these emerge. Without adequate systems, small problems can mushroom and threaten the organization before they are recognized. Management needs to realize that however good the information systems and financial controls are, they must be periodically upgraded or risk becoming obsolete.[9]

8. Strong, institution-wide motivation to grow, often stemming from moral outrage about conditions of poverty. Unless there is a critical mass of employees at all levels highly dedicated to growth, efforts to achieve rapid growth are unlikely to succeed. Most often such motivation is a product of collective indignation about the conditions of poverty and the resulting, unnecessary human suffering—conditions under which the MFI employees lived at some point in their lives. For this motivation to be deeply felt, there must be a belief among the employees that the program is having a positive impact on clients and will continue to do so; outrage without a practical plan to respond to it is not enough to sustain the required commitment over time. This motivation is necessary to see individuals and groups through the inevitable sacrifices required in the process. It must be maintained through the presence of a leader who reminds employees about the "big picture," the realities of the problem they are addressing and their ability to solve it. Fair promotion and compensation policies are also necessary. It is particularly important to provide a market-based salary structure and ensure that the organization promotes from within to the extent possible.

9. Civil peace. There is little if any record of rapid growth taking place in a country that is in the midst of a major, country-wide insurrection or civil war. However, rapid growth in microfinance has been used in post-conflict environments as an effective strategy to jumpstart economic activity.[10] Moreover, MFIs such as the Grameen Bank (1979–1982), the Integrated Development Foundation (1993–1997), and FINCA–El Salvador (early 1990s) have effectively begun operations in conditions of civil unrest or outright civil war, laying the foundation for later rapid growth.

The following are some of the nonessential but important factors that can contribute to exponential growth:

1. Competition. If an MFI coexists with another, growing MFI, this can be a strong motivator for its own growth. In the case of CRECER in Bolivia, being dismissed by the regulated MFIs as a relic of history provided strong motivation to prove them wrong, according to Chris Dunford. In addition, having a colleague MFI, Pro Mujer–Bolivia, with similar values and products helped to diffuse learning and keep the management team on its toes. Today CRECER is the second largest MFI of any type in Bolivia, measured in terms of client outreach, and it was able to avoid the political and portfolio problems that afflicted the regulated MFIs in the late 1990s (see Box 2.1). Conversely, lack of competition can stifle growth. It is easy for a single "fat and happy" MFI, in the words of one senior donor agency official interviewed for this chapter, to grow complacent and not pursue growth or product enhancement—although, as we will see with our case study in Ethiopia, this need not be the result of a noncompetitive environment.

2. Predictable and reliable financing lined up before growth is begun. While adequate financing is a requirement, having predictable, performance-based financing lined up over several years is a tremendous if rare asset for a fast-growing MFI. It frees up the MFI's CEO, who often must spend 50% to 90% of his or her time negotiating and managing financing, to focus on systems, long-range planning, increased delegation, human resources, and quality control. It also can create a sense of competition among financiers to offer better terms, thus catalyzing a self-reinforcing virtuous cycle of financial stability and decreased costs (assuming performance can be maintained). This can also spill over to benefit other MFIs, though there is some risk of a microfinance "bubble" being created in extreme cases. It is important that microfinance thought leaders do a better job of distinguishing *financing under discussion* and *firm financing commitments leading to disbursements*. Too often in microfinance, funding is discussed and even announced in a way that creates the false impression that an institution or entire sector is awash in cash, when in fact deals do not get consummated and the capital constraint remains or is even worsened as donors or investors withdraw due to perceived saturation.

3. A strong core team beyond the CEO. Second-line leadership beyond the CEO is important for effective management and for instilling confidence in external as well as internal stakeholders. Those financiers considering substantial investments in MFIs often "size up" the second tier of leadership in subtle ways as they determine the extent of their involvement. Larry Reed of

The Latin American Experience and the Case of CRECER

Clearly, the Latin American microfinance sector has provided leadership in urban applications and creating linkages to capital markets, despite its relatively low level of outreach (estimated at 2–3 million, or roughly half that of either of the two largest MFIs in Bangladesh). Members of networks with a strong presence in the region, such as ACCION International, FINCA, the Katalysis Bootstrap Fund, ProCredit, and Women's World Banking, as well as hundreds of MFIs in national-level networks, have made startling contributions to the global microfinance movement. However, with the exception of Compartamos in Mexico, there are few if any MFIs in the Latin America and Caribbean region that have grown (in terms of client outreach) at a rate comparable to that of Zakoura, ACSI, or Kashf in recent years. The Bolivian MFI CRECER, however, stands out as a promising organization that has achieved steady growth in a competitive market while demonstrating operational sustainability and staying true to its mission and target group.

Founded in 1985 as a Freedom from Hunger (FFH) nutrition program, CRECER began integrating microcredit into its health education program in 1990, and in 1999 became an independent Bolivian microfinance institution (although still part of the FFH network). Its organizational mission is to provide substantive and sustainable integrated financial and education services to poor women and their families in rural and peri-urban areas of Bolivia. As shown in the accompanying figure, CRECER's client outreach has grown from just less than 31,000 clients in 2001 to more than 74,000 clients as of January 2006. The organization reached self-sufficiency in 2001 and has maintained an impressive portfolio at risk (PAR) of less than 0.55% since 1999.

CRECER's ongoing support from FFH in the form of funding and technical assistance has certainly been a key factor in its success. Chris Dunford, president of Freedom from Hunger, explains that much of CRECER's motivation stemmed from a desire to be taken more seriously, both within the competitive Bolivian microfinance industry and among international stakeholders.

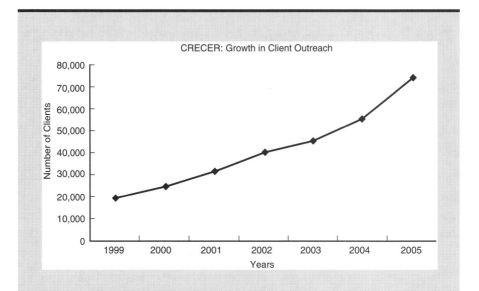

CRECER's initial outreach target was to serve 140,000 clients by 2010. Given its impressive growth in recent years, these targets are now being revisited and may be revised upward. CRECER is currently facing challenges typical of many MFIs that are gearing to scale up: developing strategies and plans in an environment where resources and financing are uncertain, as well as finding and retaining qualified staff. Dunford points out that with such uncertainty surrounding resource availability, it is difficult to decide whether to hire enough staff to manage potential future revenues, or to scale up with existing resources and risk overworking and losing staff.

Opportunity International has identified five positions beyond CEO that an MFI must fill with quality individuals in order to succeed: chief operating officer (deputy director), chief information officer, chief financial officer, product development head, and top internal auditor. Other possible positions include the top human resources officer and a critical mass of quality regional directors or the equivalent. These seem to be the key positions, though they obviously have different names in various institutions. This group needs to work effectively as a team and be supportive of the CEO, but it also should include several individuals who plausibly could take over the organization in the event of the incapacitation or resignation of the CEO.

4. Good governance and stakeholder support. MFIs embarking on rapid growth should have a reasonably well-functioning and well-qualified board of directors or the equivalent, and some kind of succession plan in place for the board chair/president and the CEO. The board and the CEO need to be committed to the organization's evolution to be able to respond to the challenges that the MFI will face over time, particularly during the scaling-up period. At a minimum, a well-functioning board is one that meets regularly (at least twice each year) and addresses issues such as budget and annual plan approval, CEO compensation, adoption of major strategic initiatives, and others called for in its by-laws, but also one that does not inappropriately involve itself in day-to-day management. Before embarking on an aggressive growth plan, it is important that the board and other stakeholders participate in the process of developing the plan, assessing and mitigating risks, and aligning actions according to a shared vision of success. As we will show, the Kashf Foundation did this at the beginning of a crucial growth spurt and, according to at least one observer, was a critical element in sustaining stakeholder support for the expansion.

5. **Products that respond to a clear need among a target population.** While it is possible to achieve growth with products that are not ideally suited to the needs of clients, such a situation reduces the likelihood of success considerably. In an environment where there are few if any alternatives available and none on the horizon, clients may put up with poorly designed products for a time. But growth is much easier if the MFI has financial products that are well designed in terms of amount, repayment schedule, social collateral requirements/mechanisms, and the application and approval process, and also if there are clear prospects for improved products and larger loans as a payment history is established. Effective and ethical marketing of financial products is critical to recruiting and retaining clients and mitigating the risk of a political backlash, as recently occurred in Andhra Pradesh, India. There should also be a clear product deployment plan for the growth phase; trying to do too much on this front can actually curtail growth. One well-designed product will go much farther than three that are flawed.

6. **Country-wide economic and monetary stability, ideally in an environment characterized by economic growth.** Maintaining a microfinance program is possible in environments of high inflation and/or recession, as evidenced by Indonesia in the late 1990s. But aggressive expansion under these conditions is probably too risky. There may be pressures to grow as part of combating macroeconomic problems, since microcredit for investment (the dominant product of most MFIs) is arguably both pro-growth and anti-inflationary, but these pressures are probably best resisted until a country's economy is on a firmer footing.

7. **Keeping management and stakeholder "perfectionism" in check.** In most, if not all, fast-growing institutions, the ability of management to ensure

high quality in every transaction is compromised as a by-product of growth. There will necessarily be a range of performance quality among staff, branches, departments, and client groups. Management and other stakeholders, such as board members and financiers, need to adjust their expectations to focus on typical performance, and avoid the temptation to hold all employees or branches to the standard of the founder or the model branch, respectively. Dr. Muhammad Yunus once said that a captain cannot show his skill on calm waters. Rapid growth is a course through high seas, and all concerned must be ready to take on some water and maybe get seasick from time to time. As long as typical performance is acceptable and poor performance is isolated, the growth process should continue.

8. Respected MFI leaders with strong ethical fiber.[11] In addition to being strong, charismatic, and skilled managers, MFI leaders who are initiating and overseeing rapid expansion (particularly those who are doing so on a scale never seen in that country) must be beyond reproach in terms of their personal and professional ethics. This quality inspires stakeholders and keeps hostile politicians at bay, particularly given the controversy that surrounds the high costs incurred by MFIs and charged to clients in many countries. An underappreciated aspect of the Bangladesh scale-up success were the well-earned reputations for personal integrity of early leaders such as Professor Yunus and Fazle Abed. Despite their being in the national and international spotlight for several decades, their honesty has never been seriously questioned. Fouad Abdelmoumni has emerged in this "microfinance statesman" role in the Arab World, and Ela Bhatt of SEWA has long played this role in India. This characteristic extends beyond the reputations of select individuals to fundamental business decisions. For example, both of the Bangladeshi MFI leaders could have exploited their early monopoly/oligopoly position for a time by charging much higher interest rates, but they chose not to do so, adopting business models focused on high volume (i.e., massive outreach) rather than high margins. This approach probably gave the Bangladesh microfinance sector, the world's most vibrant, political cover enabling its impressive growth.

Some believe that these qualities are not crucial and perhaps are even counterproductive in that they could discourage practitioners and investors from acting. This school of thought asserts that the contexts in which microfinance is succeeding vary widely and defy simple categorization and one-size-fits-all checklists. David Gibbons of Cashpor-India, for example, contends that there are really only two essential preconditions for growth: (1) sufficient potential demand from the poor and (2) the absence of major legal/regulatory obstacles. All other items cited as essential factors or preconditions in this chapter and elsewhere, Gibbons maintains, are necessary subsequent actions on the part of the MFI's management. He lists these actions as (1) cost-effective identification of poor women in their villages and working exclusively with them so as to minimize leakages to the non-poor; (2) sourcing of sufficient investment/grants/quasi-equity to finance deficits prior to financial breakeven (usually the toughest task); (3) getting commercial banks interested in the potential for earning reasonable profits by serving as wholesale lenders; (4) ensuring timely, honest, and cost-effective delivery of financial services to the poor; (5) motivating field staff with attractive, productivity-based financial incentives; (6) keeping PAR less than 5% percent; and (7) planning and monitoring financial performance to ensure breakeven at the district level within four years. Gibbons argues that putting other systems in place (such as accounts and financial reporting, Information communication technology, cash/fund management, and internal auditing) is important but relatively obvious and easy. While we do not agree with Gibbons's analysis entirely, we acknowledge that taking our analysis and recommendations too literally could discourage practitioners and investors from taking action in support of sustainable rapid-growth plans. Identifying growth-ready MFIs is certainly as much of an art as a science.

THE CASE OF FONDATION ZAKOURA

Fondation Zakoura (henceforth Zakoura) is a Moroccan MFI established in 1995. It is led by Aziz Benmaazouz, its widely respected managing director, and chaired by Noureddine Ayouch, a leading Moroccan businessman. It was one of three MFIs taking the most advantage of the more supportive regulatory environment inaugurated in 1999. It is also the one among the three that has demonstrated the strongest commitment to serving the poorest.

Morocco has approximately 4.5 million people living on less than $2/day and has 19% of its population living below the poverty line (see Table 2.1),[12] compared with 13% in 1991; the poverty rate in the rural areas is estimated at 27%.[13] In the face of this obvious need, the microfinance sector had not experienced significant growth despite the presence of a relatively progressive financial sector and no issues related to microfinance being seen as inconsistent with Islamic finance, which is not practiced in Morocco.

nual rate of 87%. Although this was a critical period in terms of the organization's groThis chapter will focus primarily on Zakoura's growth from January 2000 to December 2002, during which time it grew from 16,055 to 103,720 clients, at an average annual rate of 87%. Although this was a critical period in terms of the organization's growth, the highest growth in the percentage and number of clients occurred in years outside of this period

Table 2.1   Country Background at a Glance: Morocco

Total population	29.8 million.[i]
Level of poverty	19% living below $2 a day (PPP); poverty rate in rural areas estimated at 27%.
Microfinance demand: estimation of total market	Approximately 1.6 million, of which only 600,000 are currently being reached by 11 MFIs.[ii]
Number of MFIs	11 licensed MFIs; Zakoura and Al Amana are the largest, serving 73% of the country's active clients.
Special MFI or banking regulatory laws	The Moroccan Law on Microfinance passed in 1999, allowing MFIs to extend microcredit, lifting interest rate caps, and providing MFIs with a five-year tax break. The government prohibits MFIs from accepting savings and providing certain alternative financial services, such as micro-insurance.

[i]World Development Indicator, 2004
[ii]Estimates from Fondation Zakoura

(1998 and 2004, respectively).   According to Microfinance Information Exchange (MIX) figures covering the 1998–2004 period, Zakoura was the sixth-fastest-growing MFI in the world.[14] Although our focus is on growth through December 2002, it should be noted that as of March 2006, Zakoura had reached a total of 193,787 clients.

During the period under study, Zakoura's loan portfolio grew from $1.53 million to $15.9 million, while its operating expense ratio declined by more than one-third, from 27.59% to 17.12%. PAR remained consistently below 1%. The key growth indicators for this period are summarized in Figures 2.1 to 2.4.

Figure 2.1   Zakoura Outreach (Active Clients)

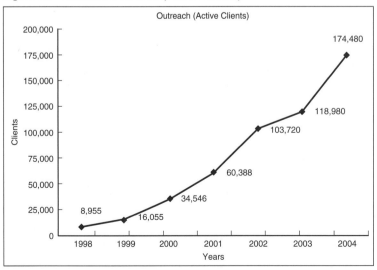

Figure 2.2   Zakoura Operating Expenses

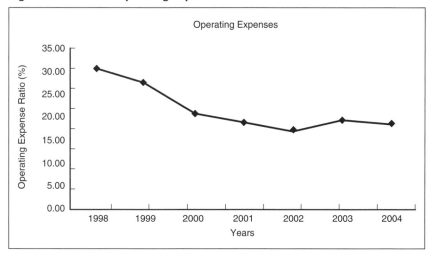

Figure 2.3   Zakoura Loans Outstanding

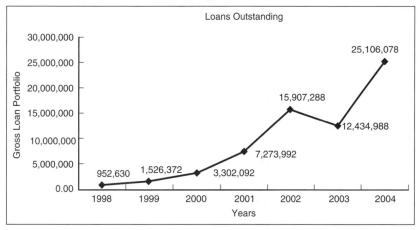

Figure 2.4   Zakoura Portfolio Quality

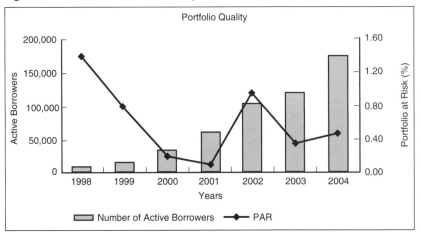

During this period, the Moroccan microfinance sector grew almost 700%, from approximately 42,000 active clients in 1999 to 297,000 in 2004, making this nation of 30 million people the microfinance leader of the Arab world. Zakoura was a major part of this growth; together with Al Amana, the two MFIs served 73% of the country's active clients.[15] Zakoura also played an important role in demonstrating that the poorest could be reached, as it targets five-member families with incomes of less than 1,500 dirhams per month, which translates to about US$1/day per capita. Zakoura's strong poverty focus is evident in many aspects of its operations. It bases its new offices in the poorest regions of Morocco as determined from the Moroccan poverty map, it conducts regular internal impact studies to ensure its effective targeting of the poor and prepares timely feedback loops concerning clients' changing poverty status, and it vigilantly tracks the client businesses' success rate in addition to its own repayment rate.

From a series of interviews with Zakoura's leadership, as well as other stakeholders and informed observers, a clear picture of the factors contributing to this achievement has emerged. These factors are summarized next.

1. Confident, risk-taking leadership. Although Zakoura has a solid second line of management, Benmaazouz and Ayouch are the key individuals. They work effectively together and have complementary roles: Benmaazouz focuses on day-to-day management of staff, and Ayouch on a few strategic initiatives such as securing financing from local banks and building a talented board of directors. Together, they exude pride, self-confidence, and a focus on reaching their goals. They embarked on a growth strategy without having ready financing or adequately developed systems. Admittedly, this was a risky approach, but they shared the belief that by starting the process they would force donors and lenders to speed up their decision making (in order to be part of the emerging success) and force staff to accelerate and simplify systems development. This was done in a context where values were not compromised and funding inconsistent with the growth strategy was not accepted. In the end, their gamble paid off. Donors and staff came through in time with financing and systems, and the organization delivered.

2. Supportive regulatory framework. The importance of the Moroccan Law on Microfinance, adopted in 1999 but effectively practiced for one or two years before that, cannot be overestimated. It legitimized microfinance, offered flexibility on interest rates that was not available to banks, and provided a tax holiday for five years. It has been amended once to allow certain types of housing loans (which were previously not allowed) but otherwise remains in force in its original form to this day. The essentials of the law, which is perhaps not ideal in every respect but are still very progressive, are as follows:[16]

- It created a new type of association (the equivalent of a 501c3 in the United States, a society in India, or a civil association in Mexico) dedicated to providing microcredit.

- It freed MFIs from the interest rate caps imposed on banks and finance companies (the Ministry of Finance retained the right to impose caps, but in practice it has not done so).

- It permitted MFIs to charge fees.

- It relieved MFIs of paying value-added taxes for five years.

- It required multipurpose NGOs to separate their financial and nonfinancial services.

- It restricted microcredit loans to productive (business-related) activities.

- It required MFIs to become financially viable within five years.

It is highly unlikely that the microfinance sector could have attracted the capital and talent needed to grow as rapidly as it did—or perhaps to grow at all—without this law being in place. While there are many studies and white papers on pro-microfinance regulation and analyses of the gaps of existing regimes, and while it is easy to criticize the gaps in this law,[17] it is important not to lose sight of the fact that the Moroccan government actually approved a law that unleashed a spurt of growth. The visionary officials who made this happen are to be congratulated and emulated, though it is important that regulations continue to evolve as the field itself evolves.[18]

3. Early willingness to take on debt. From Zakoura's earliest days, its chairman was aggressive and successful in securing interest-free loans from local banks for on-lending purposes.[19] This was important in several respects. First, it showed that the board was active and contributing in significant ways. Second, it signaled that Zakoura was sufficiently confident in its lending methodology to be willing to take on debt (and not just grants/equity) from the earliest stages of its existence. Third, it gave the senior management confidence that while there might be funding gaps of sorts, Zakoura was unlikely to be without cash for on-lending—which spurred a willingness to expand rapidly as long as operating costs could be kept low. This early decision to take on local debt, and success in doing so, distinguishes Zakoura from the other leading MFIs in Morocco.

4. Strong desire to grow fueled by moral outrage. Zakoura's staff are clearly highly motivated and work very hard. This has been widely attributed to moral outrage at the conditions of poverty and the belief that microcredit is effectively able to address this serious societal problem. Such feelings permeate the organizational culture, and while arguments based on other considerations can be made to external partners such as donors, internally the scandal of unnecessary poverty is justification enough for expansion—even risk-taking expansion that requires a degree of personal sacrifice on the part of staff. The question that is effectively posed to all staff is this: if women clients are willing to work hard and take risks in their businesses and lives as they strive to defeat poverty, why should Zakoura expect less from itself?

5. Cost-consciousness. Perhaps as a result of the uncertainty that has always characterized funding for operations and systems, Zakoura has strived to keep operating costs, especially head-office costs, low. Mark Edington of Save the Children, who worked closely with Zakoura from 1998 to 2001, contends that its penny-pinching approach has been critical to its rapid growth. One example is its policies regarding transportation for loan officers: rather than purchase vehicles, Zakoura has found that it is much cheaper and more sustainable to have the loan officers take local buses and taxis. As Edington has persuasively argued, once an organization has reached the point of employing hundreds of loan officers, every additional cost is multiplied hundreds of times. Arguably, these high costs have "starved" the organization of needed upgrades, resulted in an overworked staff (particularly those at the head office), and harmed relationships with some stakeholders (since inquiries are sometimes not responded to promptly because the head-office team is so lean). However, the organization has delivered time and again on major business plan goals despite being financially strapped, and this is probably the result of creative thinking, nonfinancial incentives for staff, and stakeholder recognition that while Zakoura is not as responsive as one might hope, it usually comes through with solid results in the end. The fact that this fiscal discipline is enforced organization-wide, even at the level of the managing director, has made it palatable and has helped keep costs under control, and in this sense it has been an important factor in ensuring the success of what would otherwise be a very risky growth strategy.

6. **Equity infusion through the Hassan II Fund.** Complementing and magnifying the impact of the microfinance law was the establishment by the Moroccan government of the Hassan II Fund in 2000. It was capitalized at $10 million and provided grants to qualified MFIs on a competitive basis, and it was fully disbursed by 2001—an impressive achievement considering how many donor and government financing vehicles become politicized and/or mired in bureaucracy that leaves resources unspent after many years. While there is some controversy about how the grants were allocated between the MFIs that were larger at the time (and much larger now) and those that were smaller, in general it can be said that this was one government initiative where formalities were streamlined, disbursements timely, and decisions made mainly if not entirely on the merits of the proposals. There were no significant strings attached that were not related to compliance with the microfinance law and attainment of growth targets. For Zakoura, this meant an infusion of equity in the amount of $3.7 million at a critical time. As the first *Pathways out of Poverty* publication persuasively argued, equity is often a key missing ingredient for MFIs that want to scale up.[20] The grants from Hassan II met this need in meaningful amounts. While grants (the closest equivalent of equity for non-profits) are often said to "crowd out" private investment and make its recipients complacent, in fact these capital injections constituted catalysts for growth, enhanced efficiencies, and increased incentives for tapping local and international capital markets. Zakoura and other MFIs were thoughtful and creative in stretching out these grants in pursuit of growth objectives.

7. **Effectiveness at securing resources and designing systems "on the fly."** Given the risky strategy of embarking on rapid growth as a way of coaxing financiers to provide funding and encouraging staff to develop simple but effective systems, it was essential that management prove that this could be done; otherwise, expansion would need to be scaled back dramatically, which would have a negative impact on morale and how Zakoura was perceived. Fortunately, management was able to deliver on its promise and prove the viability of the model. Benmaazouz asserts that if the expansion had been delayed until funds were lined up and systems developed, it might never have taken place because donors and mid-level managers would never have felt the requisite urgency to act. The key achievements in terms of securing resources and developing systems are summarized in Table 2.2.

Table 2.2   Zakoura Funding Sources and Systems Development Summary 2000–2003

Year	Major Funding Secured*	Key Systems Developed/ Revised or New Initiative Launched
2000	• Fonds Hassan II awards US$3.7 million to Zakoura for loan capital. • USAID awards 5,742,330 Moroccan dirhams (MAD) (US$570,000) to Zakoura (subsidies for investment and operations). • European Union awards 700,000 euros (US$650,000) (subsidies for investment and operations).	• Expansion into southern region of Morocco (region of Tiznit)
2001	• COOPI awards 140,000) MAD (US$13,000) and ADPPN lends 950,325 MAD (US$90,000).	• Individual loans development and lending in the branch of Nador • Lending in the city of Essaouira
2002	• CGAP awards US$220,000. • FADES awards 111,000 Kuwaiti dinars (US$364,000) (subsidies for operations). • USAID awards US$2,000,000 as a guarantee fund for housing loans.	• Developed new MIS • Established Finance Department • Established Auditing & Controlling Department • Developed housing loan policies
2003	• USAID provides US$4,000,000 as a guarantee fund for individual loans. • European Investment Bank lends 5,000,000 euros (US$5.88 million) (10-year loan term).	• Created Human Resources Department

*Excluding commercial loans.

8. **Partnership with Save the Children and Microstart.** During and prior to the period under study, Zakoura worked with Save the Children (SC) as part of the Microstart program of UNDP and UNCDF. Zakoura was by far the best performing of the six MFIs to which SC provided technical assistance

under contract. The advice and credentialing that came with the partnership were important assets to Zakoura. Also important was the fact that SC respected its partner enough to allow it to implement recommendations within a time frame and in a manner that suited its needs. They trusted that Zakoura was a fundamentally open institution seeking new ideas for improvements, and realized that Zakoura often needed time to adapt and implement a new idea to make it truly its own.

The SC-Zakoura relationship was complex, but both institutions worked hard to make it successful. Compromises and flexibility were required. Sometimes Zakoura staff would not report out to SC that they had implemented a recommendation (due to forgetfulness, pride, or both). Other technical assistance providers besides SC have been struck by how many new ideas Zakoura has been able to embrace and adopt. In an important paper reflecting on his experiences in Morocco with Microstart and MFI partners including Zakoura, Edington identified several key characteristics of an MFI with high potential to grow; among them is openness to new ideas.[21]

9. Focus on performance over marketing/positioning. Zakoura emphasized performance over marketing from the beginning. While this may have led to some missed opportunities in terms of international donor financing, Xavier Reille of CGAP contends that "it has been Zakoura's strength to focus on core business rather than frequenting conferences or courting donors." Furthermore, Reille argues that "Zakoura's growth has been rooted in Moroccan expertise and funding sources (Hassan II and commercial banks), effectively reducing dependency on often capricious donor funding." We believe that by focusing on performance and carefully screening opportunities to present its accomplishments at international seminars, Zakoura was able to carefully shepherd its human and financial resources so that most of them could be directly deployed in support of outreach goals. Being seen as focused on substance rather than marketing probably helped Zakoura in dealing with the most sophisticated donors, and perhaps even created a kind of mystique about the association. Jamii Bora, a fast-growing MFI in Kenya supported by the U.S.-based Unitus and other organizations, has similarly shunned the spotlight in growing to 100,000 clients and beyond, and seems to have benefited—or at least certainly has not been harmed—by doing so. Also noteworthy is that Zakoura never apologized for or tried to repackage (either for its microfinance clients or industry thought leaders) its group-based and targeted lending methodology, though they of course tinkered with it, as any organization would to enhance its impact and efficiency.

10. Friendly competition. While Zakoura usually did not compete directly for clients with Al Amana or Banque Populaire—as these excellent MFIs tended to focus slightly more upmarket and did not, until very recently, compete at all in the rural areas—it is undeniable that they did compete to some extent for clients with these MFIs and to a lesser degree with the eight smaller MFIs in Morocco. This had a positive effect on product development and cost containment. More important, Zakoura competed with Al Amana for thought leadership of the Moroccan microfinance movement and for partnerships with influential institutions such as CGAP, USAID, the Grameen–Abdul Latif Jameel Initiative (a collaboration between the Abdul Latif Jameel Group, a leading Saudi Arabian business conglomerate, and Grameen Foundation), the Atlanta-based Rockdale Foundation, and the Moroccan government. It is difficult to imagine Zakoura being as aggressive and creative as it was without two other fast-growing MFIs in its market. Benmaazouz has stated that when USAID opted to make a large investment in starting Al Amana rather than scaling up Zakoura, the latter took that rejection as a challenge. (Zakoura received some support from USAID, but nowhere near the amount provided to Al Amana.) Since the relationship between these MFIs was friendly and collegial, good ideas flowed among them to some extent; as a result, Zakoura did not need to invent every approach it used, but was able to adapt those pioneered by its peers in some cases. It is notable that the leaders of Al Amana and Zakoura speak highly of each other in public and in private.

Subsequent to its nearly 90% annual growth over the three years that we have focused on, Zakoura has slowed to a roughly 35% yearly increase in outreach; but as a result of having reached meaningful scale by the end of 2002, even this lower rate of expansion translates to an additional 3,400 clients per month over the period January 2003 to September 2005. This relatively slower growth and consolidation has allowed for more research and development, greater penetration into rural areas, an increased presence at industry conferences, and additional management time to ensure that systems to catch up with growth. The essence of the strategy and the values that informed it remain much the same.

THE CASE OF THE KASHF FOUNDATION

The Kashf Foundation (henceforth Kashf), established in 1996 and based in Lahore, Pakistan, was founded on the belief that the economic empowerment of women is a key factor toward the achievement of socioeconomic development in Pakistan. Of Pakistan's 148 million people, 85% live on less than $2 a day, and 35% are barely surviving on less than $1 a day (see Table 2.3).

Table 2.3   Country Background at a Glance: Pakistan

Total population	148 million (estimated)
Level of poverty	35%
Microfinance demand: estimation of total market	Approximately 50 million, out of which less than 8% have access to microfinance through institutional sources.
Number of MFIs	Fifteen major ones, and thousands of other NGOs that are involved in microfinance, out of which only about 50 are expected to reach scale in their microfinance efforts given current trends.
Special MFI or banking regulatory laws	The government passed the Microfinance Ordinance in 2001, a legal and regulatory framework to allow for licensing and regulation of specialized microfinance banks.
Other important factors	The presence of an apex or wholesale fund (Pakistan Poverty Alleviation Fund) has greatly helped the sector expand by providing access to large amounts of low-interest funding. The development of a small but effective network organization (the Pakistan Microfinance Network) is leading to adoption of best practices and learning through peer exchanges.

Access to credit for the poor is typically limited to local moneylenders, who charge as much as 350% interest per annum. There are thousands of tragic stories where poor households, facing severe financial distress, have resorted to borrowing money at these exorbitant rates and were plunged into a self-reinforcing cycle of indebtedness and destitution.

At the time of Kashf's founding, there was a large unmet need for credit among low-income households in Pakistan. The best mechanism for delivering this is a pro-poor and client-friendly microfinance organization. Kashf's group lending program has grown from 913 clients in June 1999 to 80,191 clients as of March 2006, with an outstanding portfolio of $13 million and cumulative disbursements of $57 million, making it the third largest NGO involved in microfinance in the country. Kashf has also managed to achieve financial sustainability over this period. Current outreach in the sector is about 550,000 clients, which is a mere 8% of the estimated market demand.

Figure 2.5 Kashf Outreach (Active Clients)

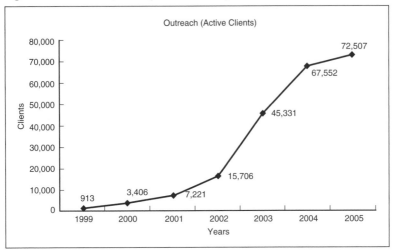

Growth Experience

Kashf's outreach grew from approximately 7,000 clients in 2001 to more than 72,000 clients in 2005. Kashf grew by 117% during the 2001–2002 fiscal year, and by 189% during 2002–2003. The growth in Kashf's client base has been managed in such a way that the PAR has been under 2% since 2001. Although the focus of this case study extends only through December 2003, as of March 2006 Kashf had reached a total of 80,259 clients.

The organization has been continuously assessing its existing and potential clients' needs and has been adapting its products to bring them in line with the changing situations and client needs. In this area, Kashf introduced emergency (consumption) loans and micro-insurance for its clients, thereby taking the lead in expanding the frontier of financial services in the Pakistani microfinance industry. There are several important contributing factors in Kashf's growth phase, such as testing and perfecting products, building an adequate human resource base, securing long-term donor support, building systems to elicit input from clients, and regularly assessing the impact of the program on clients. As these elements were being put in place, the organization deliberately grew slowly. Figure 2.5 highlights the various phases of Kashf's growth path over the past few years:

Essential Factors Supporting Growth

It is important to analyze the most important contributors to Kashf's rapid growth. The primary building blocks included the following:

1. Vision, leadership, and corporate governance. Throughout its history the organization, and particularly its senior managers and board, has maintained a focus on delivering financial services to the poor. Furthermore, the institution has always strived to articulate and follow a clear business strategy, which has evolved along with the organization. This has been strengthened by the ability of the management to communicate Kashf's mission, vision, and core values across all tiers of the institution. Third parties we spoke to repeatedly emphasized the passion for microfinance of Kashf's staff and spoke specifically of the managing director's pivotal role as the driving force and inspiration for the organization. When asked what makes Kashf stand out, Steve Rasmussen, a microfinance specialist at the World Bank, replied that it was their "absolute clarity of vision from day one."

2. Methodology and emphasis on a simple product range. Kashf Foundation employs a group lending methodology that has been refined over the last thirty years and seems especially suited to the South Asian context. The products are simple and are easy to replicate and roll out in urban communities. During the three years prior to scaling up, the organization spent a great deal of time standardizing products primarily designed to meet the needs of women from low-income communities, and it also focused on standardizing branch-level systems. Based on this extensive analysis, several changes were made in the overall product offerings. For example, research had revealed a high demand for insurance services among Kashf clients, and as a result Kashf became the first MFI in Pakistan to introduce a micro-insurance product, which covered the death risk of the client by insuring the entire amount of loan balances, along with providing a funeral benefit to the family at the time of death. However, after testing its core set of products, the organization settled on a "one-size-fits-all" delivery approach during its growth phase.

3. Maintenance of high portfolio quality. Even though portfolio quality is considered essential for any MFI, it is critical to one attempting to grow rapidly. Figure 2.6 illustrates that with the exception of 2000, Kashf's PAR has remained below 2%. The case of 2000 is important to understand; during that year the organization was severely constrained in access to funds for on-lending. Loan disbursements were intermittent, and this negatively impacted the credibility of the organization; predictably, many clients began to stop repaying loans. The importance of maintaining sufficient liquidity to meet the borrowing needs of qualified clients in a growth context, or any stage of an MFI's evolution, for that matter, is apparent.

4. Enhancing management depth and decentralizing operations. For any MFI to grow rapidly, developing highly skilled second-tier management is an important challenge. Mentoring and coaching staff, focusing on promoting from within, and inculcating sound values and ethics are important building blocks

Figure 2.6   Kashf Portfolio Quality

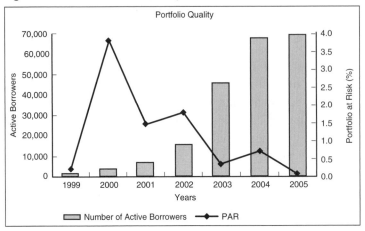

for ensuring sustainable growth. Kashf focused particularly on enhancing top management capacity and also decentralized operations by introducing field-based supervisory staff (called area managers in the Kashf system) who were charged with realizing the vision of "decentralization with adequate controls." This was combined with a strong focus on quality management and on establishing clear and transparent performance goals for all tiers. A strong system of human resource management is essential for any growing institution where staff learning, growth, and development needs are at the forefront. At this stage, Kashf especially followed the strategy of promoting staff from within.

5. **Focusing on sustainability and appropriate pricing.** It is essential for an MFI to have a clear vision to project to clients as well as institutional sustainability. This becomes even more critical when gauged against the general microfinance context in which it operates. In the Pakistani environment in particular, microfinance continues to be seen by many as a welfare-oriented tool.[22] Even policymakers have tried to fit it into the poverty alleviation/charity paradigm. As a result, one of the first challenges Kashf faced was finding a price for its service that would make the program sustainable within five years after the conclusion of a two-year action-research period. This strategy enabled the program to establish sound financial practices within the market and to build its own financial resources over time (see Figure 2.7).

6. **Ensuring optimal use of grants and subsidies in the context of developing long-term, mutually beneficial relationships with donors.** The availability of training/exposure opportunities and grant funds in the initial stages, perhaps none more important than those provided by Grameen Trust, plus the long-term strategic support from donors like the Aga Khan Foundation (AKF) and the Department for International Development (DFID), were critical in allowing Kashf to build internal capacity and set up infrastructure

Figure 2.7   Kashf Sustainability

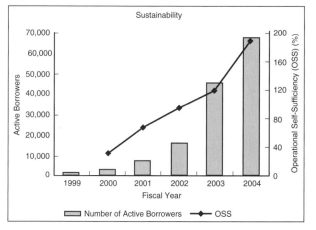

for the rapid-growth phase (see Figure 2.8). The importance of long-term support from donors that hold the organization accountable to big-picture goals cannot be emphasized enough, particularly in holding the organization responsible for the financial bottom line and maintaining its poverty focus. As mentioned earlier in the chapter, this allowed the managing director to focus on operational issues rather than on fund-raising. The role of CGAP was also important. It instilled a strong financial discipline and stressed the overarching need for financial transparency at all levels by providing a flexible grant to Kashf ahead of the growth phase. The important feature of this relationship was that Kashf had to enhance its outreach and financial performance, which shows that donors with the correct tools for accountability can actually enable an organization to grow faster. Other innovative relationships that sparked growth and innovation included the organization's ongoing relationship with Grameen Foundation through access to long-term loans denominated in local currency. (Kashf also received Grameen Foundation's prestigious Pioneer award in 2002, which enhanced its reputation internationally.)

However, it's important to note here that the organization did not pass on this subsidy to clients by providing below-market interest rates, but instead used it as "quasi-equity" to build an institutional base and to improve systems and procedures and to develop a cohesive, pro-poor organizational culture. One way of measuring this is to see how the efficiency indicators behaved over the rapid-growth period, and how the equity base was built up. As shown in Figure 2.7, the organization was able to achieve 120% operational self-sufficiency (OSS) by 2003 along with reducing its administrative costs from 72% in 2000 to 21% in 2003, as a result of productivity gains on several fronts. The income generated from loans over the same period grew at

Figure 2.8   Kashf Financing Breakdown

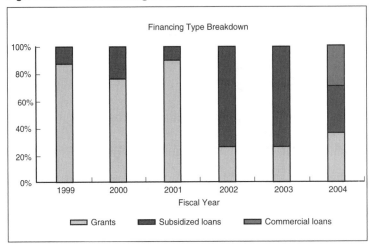

an annual rate of 240%, amounting to approximately $1 million, which could be redeployed in the program as "quasi-equity."

7. **Delighting clients and establishing strong learning principles.** Innovation and customer focus has helped Kashf evolve its products to suit client needs, giving it a competitive advantage. In Pakistan, Kashf has been a pioneer in several areas. As mentioned earlier, it was the first in its market to experiment with micro-insurance and emergency loans, and will soon be the first Pakistani MFI to offer a home improvement loan to its clients. Innovation and learning involves a certain degree of risk taking, which in turn requires strong leadership and long-term external stakeholders willing to invest "patient capital" (financial and technical). Kashf has established long-term relationships with leading MFIs in other markets (including Grameen Bank and ASA in Bangladesh) to support the improvement of its systems, policies, and procedures so that resources were not wasted on reinventing the wheel. Central to the organizational culture was inculcating the humility necessary to recognize and learn from institutional mistakes and share the lessons openly with stakeholders. We believe that this aspect of Kashf served it well as it prepared for and launched its aggressive expansion.

8. **Establishing a focused market niche.** Kashf's management maintained a clear focus in terms of its market niche—clearly defined in its business plan as "women from low-income households." This approach has been one of the key strengths of the program, for, as in other countries and regions, women have demonstrated better reliability and greater willingness to participate in microfinance programs than their male counterparts. However, the approach followed by Kashf has been to lend to poor households through women, and therefore it has not insisted that women clients use the loans exclusively if that is not what

the family considers the most logical investment strategy. This degree of flexibility allows women to participate in the program and men and women to mutually agree where the loan capital will be spent, and it has been a primary reason for the success of the program and for its widening outreach.

9. Refining the growth model. The choice the organization makes in how it will open new branches and target new markets is important. Throughout its growth phase, Kashf followed an expansion model that was based on setting up fully staffed branches in areas identified as having large numbers of people who were likely to desire its products. To keep costs down, branches normally did not serve clients outside of a 5–10-kilometer radius; this required careful selection of branch sites to ensure adequate demand. At the same time, efficiency and the importance of keeping costs down was a key accountability tool for which the branch managers and area managers were held responsible. This level of participation from all tiers actually allowed the organization to bring down costs as measured in terms of administrative efficiency from 72% in 2000 to 21% in 2003—which is noteworthy since many fast-growing MFIs are unable to increase efficiency until after they stabilize at higher outreach levels.

10. The availability of on-lending funds. As mentioned in an earlier case study, access to performance-based on-lending funds was critical during this period. The government, inspired by the experiences of Grameen Bank and PKSF in Bangladesh, worked with the World Bank to set up the Pakistan Poverty Alleviation Fund (PPAF) in 1999. PPAF functions as a wholesale fund for MFIs in Pakistan and quickly became a major source of funds for the sector, including Kashf. As Figure 2.8 shows, in 2002 and 2003 there was a heavy reliance by the organization on low-interest loans from PPAF (which lends at 6%). The role of PPAF in the growth of MFIs such as Kashf was very important; however, in our view there is room for improving the service of PPAF so that it is more responsive to the changing needs of Pakistani MFIs, though this is a topic beyond the scope of this chapter.

11. Growing in proximity. Earlier sections emphasized the need for a focused business strategy that clearly defines the market niche, the products, and the delivery methodology. One very important aspect of this growth strategy in the case of Kashf was the plan to grow in proximity to the Lahore market. The first 18 months of the growth phase focused on building outreach in Lahore. The city of Lahore alone has a population of 6 million people, 1.2 million of whom are poor. However, the level of penetration of MFIs in Lahore even today is estimated to be 75,000 households, or approximately 31% of the potential target size. In the latter half of the growth phase, the organization focused on entering new markets and other districts that were in close proximity to Lahore, thus keeping a strong check on costs and limiting its exposure to the risks that come with managing far-flung operations.

12. The Pakistan Microfinance Network and sectoral transparency. The Zakoura case study illustrates the importance of friendly competition reflecting shared principles of microfinance delivery. The way that this worked in Pakistan was through the Pakistan Microfinance Network (PMN), which was started informally in 1997. MFIs from all over the country began to share information and lessons learned, and soon benchmarks began to emerge for the industry as a whole. This process actually helped Kashf to compare itself against the entire vista of the microfinance industry in the country and motivated the organization to scale up in order to demonstrate the possibility of rapid growth in the context of the sector in Pakistan. However, Khawar Ansari, chair of the Kashf board, believes that the *lack* of competition at the initial stage allowed Kashf to pursue its strategic plan with a singular focus and without distraction.

It is important to take stock of how things could have been done differently, and perhaps more effectively, during the growth phase. It may have helped the organization if branch procedures and processes were automated earlier, but the process was delayed as Kashf struggled to develop its own software. (Buying an off-the-shelf product likely would have been a sounder approach.) If Kashf had limited its growth to Lahore and only one other district, rather than three, in the first year of the growth spurt, some quality control problems could have been prevented and the second phase of growth completed sooner. Arguably, Kashf should have built stronger networks with the financial sector by borrowing more and earlier from commercial sources. Another lesson learned concerned the process of branch opening. In retrospect, Kashf should have listened to advisors who recommended that branch opening be a regular monthly process, rather than being concentrated into two discrete periods in the year, an approach that put too much pressure on the staff and systems.

Following the rapid period of growth, 2005 was seen as the year of taking stock and ensuring that previous growth was maintained and gaps in program implementation narrowed by refraining from adding branches that year. The number of branch units had tripled in a period of three years, and a more cohesive approach had to be designed to minimize institutional risks; this included improving second-tier management in the field, reducing staff attrition, handling area-specific delinquency, reducing communication gaps between the field and the head office, and improving financial management. The organization is now poised for growth once again and hopes to maintain a 50% growth rate over the next four years and to reach 500,000 clients by 2009.

THE CASE OF AMHARA CREDIT AND SAVINGS INSTITUTION

Amhara Credit and Savings Institution (ACSI) began in 1996 as a pilot program of the Organization for the Rehabilitation and Development of Amhara (ORDA), an indigenous NGO originally established to provide relief to those affected by drought and war in the Amhara region of Ethiopia. ACSI was licensed as a microfinance share company in April 1997, and in due course it became one of the leading MFIs in the country. ACSI's primary mission is to improve the economic situation of poor people in the Amhara region by providing increased access to lending and saving services.

Ethiopia: Country Background

Of Ethiopia's 71 million inhabitants, nearly 81% live on less than $2 a day, and 26.3% barely survive on less than $1 a day (see Table 2.4). The supply of formal financial services is woefully inadequate. Studies indicate that less than 1% of the rural population has access to formal financial services of any kind.[23] The traditional alternative for many Ethiopians has been to borrow from the *Arata Abedari* (moneylenders), where interest rates typically range between 120% and 240%, although, according to a recent IFAD study, these rates can run as high as 400% per annum.[24]

The need for microfinance is urgent, and the local practitioners are beginning to respond. Since the implementation of a microfinance law in 1996, the sector has grown significantly. Twenty-six licensed MFIs were serving some 1.21 million clients as of 2005.[25] In spite of recent growth, meeting the overwhelming demand remains a challenge that MFIs are struggling to meet.

ACSI is one of the few microfinance institutions operating in the rural areas of Amhara, one of the poorest regions of Ethiopia. A 2004 study by the Central Statistical Authority in Ethiopia found that more than 30% of the 18 million people in Amhara cannot afford to maintain the minimum caloric consumption for survival.[26] Agriculture dominates the economy in Amhara, providing employment to more than 87% of its population.[27] Thus, the vast majority of ACSI loans are related to agriculture. Agricultural lending, risky and costly under the best circumstances, is especially challenging in Amhara. Much of the land suffers from environmental degradation, and the region is prone to drought and famine. Farmers do not rely on modern farming technology, and there is no effective irrigation system in place. The region's poor infrastructure, especially in the areas of transportation and telecommunications, renders many ACSI areas inaccessible. An estimated 80% of the roads in Amhara become impassable during the rainy season.

Table 2.4   Country Background at a Glance: Ethiopia

Total population	71 million (estimated)
Level of poverty	81% living under $2 a day (PPP), 26.3% living under $1 a day (PPP)
Microfinance demand: estimation of total market	13.4 million, of which only 9% are currently being helped by Ethiopia's licensed MFIs
Number of MFIs	26 licensed MFIs, serving a total of 1.21 million clients
Special MFI or banking regulatory laws	The Ethiopian Microfinance Law was adopted in 1994, allowing MFIs to provide microcredit as well as collect and mobilize public savings, and has been amended several times since 1994

Amha, Wolday. "Managing the Growth of Microfinance Institutions to Reach Large Number of Clients: Experience from Ethiopia." Amha states that 9% of microfinance demand is met by the twenty-six licensed MFIs, which are reaching a combined 1.21 million clients. The authors thus deduced that the estimated market demand for microfinance is approximately 13.4 million people.

Taking into account the daunting obstacles faced by rural MFIs in Ethiopia, ACSI's dramatic growth is all the more impressive. With 434,694 active clients in 2005,[28] up from just over 150,000 in 2001, ACSI has become the largest microfinance institution in Ethiopia (see Figure 2.9). Through a network of 10 branches and 175 sub-branches, ACSI had a loan portfolio of $54 million and a savings balance of $28.9 million.

Figure 2.9   ACSI Profile: Outreach and PAR

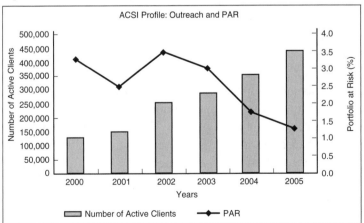

Although it reached a peak of 67% in 2002, ACSI's growth rate has been fairly constant and impressive over the last five years. This case study examines ACSI's expansion over the four-year period spanning 2001 to 2005. During this time, ACSI nearly tripled in size while maintaining a repayment rate of at least 99% and, perhaps most impressive, an operating expense ratio under 10%. Although the period under study ends in December 2005, it is worth noting that as of April 2006, ACSI's client outreach totaled 446,625.[29]

What explains ACSI's success over this period? A careful review of their experience revealed the following contributors to its growth, along some additional factors related to its success.

1. Overwhelming demand in an underserved market. There is seemingly no limit to the number of potential ACSI clients. The estimated demand for microfinance services in the Amhara region is 2.9 million.[30] ACSI, even with its extensive outreach, meets only 15% of this demand.[31] Unlike the cases of Kashf and Zakoura, ACSI has very little competition in its area of operation; the majority of licensed MFIs in Ethiopia are working primarily in urban and peri-urban areas. Three other MFIs operate in a few of the same *woredos* (districts) as ACSI, but serve a combined clientele of approximately 10,000. Saving and Credit Cooperatives (SACCOs) have minimal outreach in rural areas; recent surveys suggest that the total membership of SACCOs in the Amhara region is less than 7,000.[32]

Although lack of competition is often associated with stunted growth and inefficiency, this has not been the case with ACSI. In the absence of significant competition, ACSI has operated at a high level of efficiency and continues to push itself to reach more clients with greater effectiveness and impact. ACSI demonstrates that the external pressure to provide better services with greater efficiency, which is typically created by competition, can also be generated from within. It appears that ACSI treats the condition of poverty itself as a "competitor" that must be beaten. ACSI has operationalized this philosophy by setting clear strategies and challenging targets to drive innovation and growth.

2. Shared vision, commitment, and drive of staff. A dedicated staff embracing a common mission is critical to the success of any MFI, and ACSI satisfies this condition. As is the case with Zakoura and Kashf, ACSI staff willingly work long hours, fueled by moral outrage at the persistent poverty in their communities and by the belief in microfinance's power to improve these conditions. Staff at all levels of the organization share what Dr. Wolday Amha, director of the Association for Ethiopian Microfinance Institutions (AEMFI), describes as ACSI's "broad vision," in which performance expectations are set very high. The achievement of reaching 434,000 clients by December 2005 was based on an aggressive goal to reach 600,000 by that point. The entire organization seems motivated to reach that goal during 2006.

3. Enabling regulatory environment. The microfinance law passed in 1994 by the Ethiopian government proved vital to the growth not only of ACSI, but of the country's entire microfinance sector. The new law authorized microfinance institutions not only to provide microcredit, but also to mobilize public savings and to draw and accept bank drafts. The minimum capital required for a license was set at a low 200,000 birr ($23,256) to encourage new entrants; compare this with the 20 million rupees ($500,000) required for incorporation as a non-bank finance company MFI in India. MFIs were also declared exempt from paying income and sales taxes. In 1998 interest rate ceilings were lifted, and the task of determining appropriate interest rates was delegated to the boards of MFIs. The law was further relaxed in 2002, when the Central Bank of Ethiopia (CBE) passed a directive that increased loan ceilings, extended allowable loan terms to two years, and lowered the minimum interest rate paid on deposits from 7% to 3%.

While it is clear that the supportive regulatory environment has made it possible for MFIs such as ACSI to operate and continue to grow, there are several areas in the microfinance law that could be improved upon. Many argue that certain aspects of the CBE's regulatory framework have limited the scope of MFI services.[33] For example, the minimum interest rate paid to depositors, though lower than that in many other countries, is still high enough that it makes it difficult for MFIs working in remote regions to cover their costs. As a result, many MFIs are discouraged from entering the more remote and inaccessible regions entirely. The imposed maximum loan term of two years, relaxed in 2002 from one year, makes it difficult if not impossible for MFIs to provide housing loans. Yet overall, the regulatory framework is quite progressive and reflects a commitment on the part of the government to promote microfinance.

4. Collection and mobilization of savings. The ability to collect and mobilize savings has been a critical component of ACSI's impressive growth. ACSI currently provides savings services to more than 480,000 clients, and as of December 2005 it had a savings balance of almost $29 million. In 2002 deposits composed 44% of ACSI's total assets, and thus financed a significant portion of its outstanding loan portfolio. ACSI's heavy reliance on savings to finance growth has given it a significant degree of financial independence. ACSI executive director Mekonnen Yelewem wessen explained, "ACSI sees savings as its only sustainable source of funding in the long term. Commercial funding is not easily available, clients' demand is not fully met, and ACSI needs more funds to finance planned growth."[34] Sharing his own insights on the necessary preconditions for growth, Professor Yunus echoed Mr. Yelewem wessen's statement when he recently said, "Money does not have to come from outside. Deposit-taking and the creation of regulatory authority [to allow for it] are the real answers."

Figure 2.10   ACSI Funding Sources

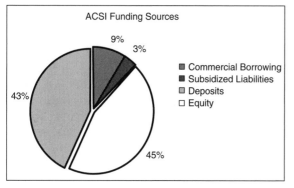

ACSI Funding Sources

- Commercial Borrowing
- Subsidized Liabilities
- Deposits
- Equity

9%
3%
43%
45%

5. Generous donor funding and strategic injection of equity. The importance of donor funding in financing ACSI's growth is apparent from Figure 2.10, which shows that 43% of ACSI's funding comes from its own equity. Of this amount, more than 60% has come in the form of donated capital from international agencies such as the Swedish International Development Agency (SIDA) and UNDP, as well as a number of Ethiopian agencies. ACSI has enjoyed consistent support from several donors over the years, most notably SIDA, which has provided grants totaling almost $6 million over the last eight years. As ACSI has grown and reached self-sufficiency, donor funding has decreased, as expected. Yet ACSI has maintained close relationships with its donors, whose assistance now comes mostly in the form of financing to support capacity building.

6. Support from regional government. ACSI has benefited from its close ties to the Amhara State Regional Government, which owns 25% of the organization's shares (the remaining 75% is owned by local NGOs and development associations). Ethiopia's Rural Development Strategy in 2001 specified the government's priority of reversing the country's culture of dependency on international aid, and microfinance—with its built-in orientation to self-sufficiency and income generation—has emerged as an important part of the strategy to realize this vision. As a result, ACSI has become a key partner of the federal and local governments. One benefit of this alliance has been the willingness of government agencies to make their buildings available to ACSI for use as sub-branches.

Although ACSI has clearly benefited from its relationship with the government, such close ties also present challenges. Because it is one of the only microfinance institutions in Amhara, the regional government has often tried to use ACSI as a vehicle to carry out its own programs. For example, the local government has in the past provided funds to ACSI to manage a lending program focused on agricultural inputs. While this has proven to be a profitable and low-risk venture for ACSI (since the local government guaranteed the loans), it has taken some of ACSI's attention away from its target clientele and undermined its autonomy.

Another challenge ACSI faces as a result of its close government ties is pressure regarding its interest rates. ACSI currently charges 18% (calculated on a declining balance), which is low compared with the rates of international MFIs. Still, ACSI management is constantly defending its rate to local government officials and others, who believe it to be far too high a rate to charge to the poor.

ACSI management has recently taken concrete steps to assert their independence. They have moved out of almost all the government-subsidized sub-branches and have drastically reduced the number of agricultural input loans they manage.

7. Local customization of group lending methodology. The Group Guarantee Lending Model is the dominant methodology of ACSI, and it has been found to be well suited to rural Ethiopia. ACSI management credits the group structure as one of the key factors contributing to its rapid growth and excellent repayment rate. In addition to the benefits of empowerment and social cohesion that group lending can provide to a client, the methodology also brings advantages to the organization. Not only is it a powerful form of insurance against default, but service delivery is inexpensive, allowing the MFI to serve and handle more clients at lower cost.

Equally important to ACSI's success has been its ability to customize the group lending methodology to meet the needs of clients. ACSI adaptations to the system include discontinuing the practice of holding weekly center meetings, due to Amhara's low population density and the related difficulty of assembling large numbers of people. This was coupled with a system allowing clients to withdraw compulsory savings upon the repayment of each loan, a policy that was found to substantially reduce the rate of client attrition.

8. Support from the community and tapping local knowledge. Another key to ACSI's expansion has been its enlistment and support of local communities. In every new *kebele* (village) entered, ACSI forms a six-member Credit and Savings Committee made up of local leaders, respected community members, and one ACSI employee. This committee is responsible for screening potential clients. Committee members receive training and are instructed to give priority to the poorest qualifying applicants, women, and those they know to be honest. This system, employed by MFIs throughout Ethiopia, is effective in leveraging local knowledge and resources to identify the poorest families that are likely to succeed as microfinance clients. It has also contributed greatly to ACSI's high repayment rate by providing an additional layer of social collateral: clients late on their repayments receive visits not only from the loan officer, but also from members of the Credit and Savings Committee. The unpaid committee members also take on much of the workload traditionally assumed by loan officers, thus maximizing the field worker's time and increasing staff efficiency. This innovative system works especially well in areas with little competition. Although ACSI does not foresee serious competition in the next several years, they do anticipate that at some point, when competition heats up, they may have to pay the committee members for their services, which could significantly increase operational costs.

9. Operational efficiency and cost-consciousness. ACSI has managed to maintain a low operating expense ratio (OER). During the years of rapid growth (2001–2005), its OER decreased from 9.9% to 6% (see Figure 2.11). In an August 2005 rating of ACSI, MicroRate stated, "ACSI is extremely efficient, reporting an operating expense ratio of 6 percent. This level of operational efficiency is unprecedented and far surpasses anything MicroRate has seen in Africa or Latin America. The average operating expense ratio for African MFIs rated by MicroRate is 44 percent. In Latin America it is 25 percent".[35] ACSI's level of efficiency is especially noteworthy given the amount of manual accounting it does and the great distances field workers must travel to meet clients. Despite these obstacles, the average caseload of loan officers increased from 156 to 372 between 2001 and 2005.[36]

Part of this is due to an institution-wide commitment to cost containment. Electricity is used sparingly (many sub-branch offices do not even have electricity or telephone lines), vehicles for staff are rarely used, and salaries are kept reasonably low, particularly for the field staff, who constitute two-thirds of ACSI's entire workforce.[37] Furthermore, as mentioned previously, the uncompensated services provided by the Credit and Savings Committees have also helped minimize costs.

Figure 2.11   ACSI Operating Expense Ratio

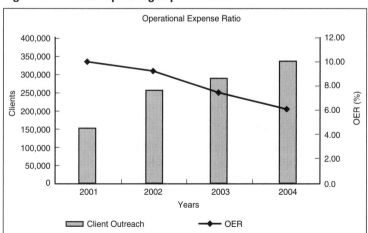

10. Recruitment, selection, and training of staff. ACSI places a high priority on recruitment, selection, and training of its staff. The lack of transportation, infrastructure, and Internet connectivity in the rural areas makes working conditions for the field staff particularly trying and staff recruitment a challenge. In such an environment, ACSI has found that local people often make excellent field staff. Not only are these people familiar with the region, people, and local culture, but they are also accustomed to the harsh work and living conditions and are therefore less likely to leave the organization.

ACSI generally promotes from within its own ranks and is therefore a strong advocate of staff training and education. In 2001, at the outset of this period of rapid growth, ACSI established a new staff development program that improved upon the training they received as part of their orientation and included new programs such as refresher training and promotional training. ACSI also created a system allowing top employees to attend summer courses at nearby universities at ACSI's expense.

At the same time, ACSI introduced a performance-based incentive system for employees. Staff members were previously eligible for standard salary increases once every two years, regardless of performance. In 2001 annual reviews of all employees based on individual and branch achievement were implemented. Promotions, salary increases, and academic scholarships were directly linked to the performance review process. This shift to a results-oriented incentive and staff development program served to further motivate and encourage the workforce, which clearly contributed heavily to ACSI's subsequent leap in client outreach.

11. Committed leadership. ACSI owes much of its success in growth to its strong and capable management team, headed by founder and executive director Mekonnen Yelewem wessen and supported by the Monitoring and Planning Department head, Getaneh Gobezie. Mekonnen Yelewem wessen assumed his current role of managing director in 2001, taking over from co-founder Tadese Kassa (now chairman of the board). Much of ACSI's subsequent growth spurt can be attributed to the organizational policies put in place in 2001—including the staff training and performance-based incentive programs mentioned above. Yelewem wessen's educational background in finance and professional experience as an accountant and auditor have been important assets to the institution. In 2001 he raised the effective interest rate from 12% to 18%, despite strong external pressure to do the opposite. The decision was extremely controversial and is one he has had to continually defend, but one we believe was necessary to ensure organizational sustainability. Yelewem wessen's ability to balance long-term financial objectives with client-level impact and outside pressures has been a critical factor in ACSI's success to date.

Remaining Challenges

Despite its tremendous strides and impressive growth, ACSI still faces a number of obstacles. The most immediate challenge is the absence of an automated and effective management information system. As mentioned earlier, management information systems are necessary to ensure the timely and accurate flow of information, and the lack of such systems can impair portfolio quality and other areas of organizational performance, including risk management. ACSI currently operates using a manual system. Records are kept by hand and transferred from the sub-branch to the branch offices, and then to the head office. ACSI management is keenly aware of this deficit and, with the financial support of USAID and SIDA, is in the process of implementing an in-house MIS that they hope will be operational by mid-2006.

ACSI also struggles to maximize its contribution to the empowerment of women. It has set a goal of reaching a client base of 50% women, yet it has consistently fallen short of this target. The percentage of women clients actually decreased between 2001 and 2004, from 38% to 29%. In addition to cultural resistance to giving women credit, the women themselves are often reluctant to form groups. Particularly in the more rural and remote areas, women are quite isolated from other households and therefore do not have much contact with other women with whom they could form groups. In contrast, men are often outside the home and involved in community activities, and thus are able to form groups with greater ease.

The challenge of reaching women clients is not unique to ACSI, but is confronted by almost all MFIs in Ethiopia. The average proportion of female clients among the sixteen largest MFIs in 2004 was 44%.[38] ACSI management maintain that they are committed to reaching women and point to the rise in female clients during the last year from 29% to 37% as evidence of the organization's renewed commitment and improved performance in this area.

Finally, ACSI still faces significant challenges in setting an interest rate compatible with political realities and long-term institutional self-reliance and financial health. A study conducted in 1996 indicated that, given the infrastructural setup in rural Ethiopia, an annual real rate of 30% to 35% would be appropriate.[39] Another study, conducted in 2000, suggests that ACSI increase its interest rate to 20–30%.[40] ACSI management will need to continue to work hard to balance all of these pressures by, among other things, keeping transaction costs low and maintaining its independence from the government.

We feel reasonably confident that ACSI will rise to meet these and other challenges, as one of ACSI's greatest strengths is its constant pursuit of improvement through honest self-appraisal. The staff and management do not try to conceal their mistakes and shortcomings from outsiders, but endeavor to address them directly and use them as learning opportunities. Their success in not only overcoming the obstacles of working in rural Ethiopia, but reaching more than 400,000 clients in eight years, is a testament to their strength and learning culture, and bodes well for the future of this impressive institution.

CONCLUSION

We live in a world plagued by a poverty crisis, one that calls out for solutions that can be scaled over time to ensure the achievement of the Millennium Development Goals. Microfinance has emerged as a powerful antipoverty strategy based on a growing body of empirical research on client-level and society-level impact. If done right, microfinance can alleviate the deprivations that poor households face and can provide them with opportunities for a better life. It is against this backdrop that the importance of scaling microfinance becomes apparent as a critical global priority, even as other breakthrough development strategies—many of which work synergistically with this one—are being improved and expanded. The identification of growth-ready MFIs, like those profiled in this chapter, and the strategic support of their business plans by other institutions, must be a central part of this effort. Also essential is the creation of enabling policy environments and the continuing refinement and improvement of product offerings, as well as the expansion of depth of outreach to ensure that the primary beneficiaries of growth are those who are poorest. Many actors have roles in supporting this process. The implications of this chapter's findings are summarized next for seven groups of stakeholders.

1. **Microfinance managers and boards:** MFIs and their leadership need to carefully assess their capacity to grow, bearing in mind the lessons in this chapter and those within the microfinance movement. They must make an effort to think like their stakeholders and, in some cases, put product innovation on hold as they begin to grow rapidly. Rapid growth requires a singular focus, and unnecessary distractions must be minimized. The needs of existing and potential clients must remain paramount, and effective targeting of the poorest should be a priority to the extent that MFIs are seeking to contribute to and benefit from resources set aside to support the achievement of the Millennium Development Goals. Cascading management functions, decentralizing decisions with adequate controls, and generating accountability through succession planning are characteristics common to all three case study subjects.

2. Regulators and policymakers: Creating a favorable policy environment for microfinance should be a priority of government in all countries where poverty persists. The recognition that microfinance is fundamentally different from traditional banking in several key respects should inform regulatory decision making. There are opportunities to learn from countries such as those that are home to the institutions profiled in this chapter. Unreasonable barriers preventing quality MFIs from securing funding, including funding from depositors, should be eliminated. The relatively high interest rates charged by MFIs should not be politicized; at the same time efforts should be made to ensure that, within a reasonable time frame, all MFIs are able to realize efficiencies and reduce rates to their cost of funds plus no more than 15–18% while remaining financially sustainable.

3. Financial institutions. Commercial financiers should follow the lead of banks such as Citigroup, Deutsche Bank, and ICICI Bank and set up business groups to explore opportunities in microfinance, drawing on the lessons learned through their philanthropic investments wherever possible. Emphasis should be placed on long-term business considerations, including establishing relationships with poor and formerly poor families and earning reasonable profits. Alliances with specialized microfinance institutions should be the primary means of developing this new customer base, with financial institutions often playing the role of wholesale lender. Equity investments are critically needed to ensure growth, continued MFI borrowing from commercial sources, and the willingness of microfinance managers to pass on cost savings to clients. Financial institutions as well as social investors should seek ways to provide equity to for-profit MFIs; this will require reasonable dividends and some degree of clarity on exit strategies. We need to focus the minds of financial experts on ensuring that currency risks are minimized for everyone involved in these transactions.

4. Donor agencies. Official aid as well as private funding should be focused on providing flexible support for systems, product innovation, research and development, managing currency risk, and other critical long-term investments in growth-ready MFIs, particularly in cases where loan capital is available from commercial sources. Another priority should be to create enabling environments through dialogue with developing-country policymakers, highlighting positive examples such as Bangladesh, Pakistan, Ethiopia, and Morocco.

5. The media. Journalists should cover the emerging microfinance success story while also giving thoughtful treatment to the remaining challenges and limitations of the model. Simplistic coverage of interest rates that can incite opposition to microfinance should be avoided, as should overselling the potential of microfinance and giving the impression that all clients succeed in overcoming poverty.

6. Researchers. Documenting the impact of a new generation of MFIs, or ones that have reinvented themselves, such as Grameen Bank, should be a research priority. Furthermore, the time lag between data collection and publication of preliminary findings should be reduced. The topic of this chapter should be revisited in a few years, as this is a fast-changing field. While we believe we have accurately captured the issues as of mid-2006, there is no telling whether they will still be representative of the state of things in a few years time. Linkages between poverty and microfinance on the one hand, and other key issues of our time, such as environmental degradation, AIDS, war, terrorism, immigration, civil unrest, sectarian conflict, and population pressures, should be explored in a new wave of studies. Another priority should be documenting the ways in which the microfinance network/infrastructure/ platform has been and can be used to realize other objectives, such as provision of telecommunications services, breaking down the digital divide, providing health education and services, ensuring high educational attainment among children of poor families, combating adult illiteracy, and full democratic participation.

7. The general public. In developed countries, where microfinance has a limited but critical role to play in addressing relative poverty and economic exclusion, the public can think and act globally by supporting one or more international microfinance networks as donors and volunteers. In their roles as consumers they can opt for products where microentrepreneurs (locally or internationally) are involved in the value chain and are fairly compensated for their contributions. In developing countries, the non-poor public can seek ways to do business with poor micro-entrepreneurs and the organizations that serve them, and support politicians and members of the media that, through their actions, support the establishment and periodic refinement of an enabling environment that seeks to benefit ethical, poverty-focused MFIs and the families they serve.

There is much to do in the years ahead if microfinance is to reach its full potential. In the words of eBay founder and noted philanthropist Pierre Omidyar, that potential extends well beyond simply reducing poverty, to "promoting full economic, social and political empowerment" on a massive scale. The possibilities have been demonstrated by pioneering institutions and individuals, including those profiled in this chapter. The actions that are needed to realize the potential of microfinance are reasonably clear. Now it is up to each of us to respond with the urgency required. There is not a moment to lose.

Notes

1. For the purposes of this chapter, "poor" refers to those living on less than $2/day per capita (adjusted for PPP) and/or below their nation's poverty line, and "the poorest" are those living on less than $1/day per capita (adjusted for PPP) and/or in the bottom half of those living below the national poverty line.
2. With an estimated $50 billion in official development assistance disbursed each year, the Consultative Group to Assist the Poor (CGAP) estimates that between $500 million and $1.5 billion goes to microfinance. The inability to estimate expenditures on microfinance more rigorously is itself a reflection of the low priority placed on microfinance despite its impressive track record and potential.
3. World Bank, *World Development Indicators 2005.*
4. UNDP, *Human Development Report 1995,* p. iii.
5. This matter of impact is documented in the Grameen Foundation white paper *Measuring the Impact of Microfinance: Taking Stock of What We Know.* This paper is available for free download from Grameen Foundation's website, http://www.gfusa. org/pubdownload/~pubid=29.
6. It should be noted that regulations that inhibit the growth of microfinance extend well beyond banking regulations to laws and policies on taxation, consumer protection, NGO regulation, securities law, and corporate regulation, as well as the many laws that affect micro-entrepreneurs themselves.
7. Among the hundreds of MFIs that visited Bangladesh and gained significant insights into how to start or scale operations, four noteworthy examples are CARD (Philippines), SHARE (India), LAPO (Nigeria), and Compartamos (Mexico), one of the leading affiliates of ACCION International, the respected U.S.-based intermediary that has decades of experience in Latin America and is now active in Africa and India.
8. A manual system can take the organization up to a certain level; however, if the organization is planning to scale up to the next stage, it needs to harness the efficiencies of technology. In other words, a manual system can handle up to 100,000 clients in a simple one- to two-product system; however, as the MFI enters new markets and grows more decentralized, from the points of view of decision making and financial health, technology becomes very important.
9. For an excellent, free toolkit related to MFI management information systems, visit www.gfusa.org/pubdownload/~pubid=24.
10. Proceedings of a conference on microfinance in post-disaster and post-conflict situation can be viewed and downloaded at http://www.gfusa.org/programs/tsunami_initiative/tsunami_conference/.
11. This quality has been identified by Bill Drayton, the founder of Ashoka, as one of the five essential characteristics of a social entrepreneur.
12. UNDP, *Human Development Report,* 2005.
13. UNDP, *Human Development Report,* 2005.
14. Growth is measured in percentage terms. The top five (in order) were SKS, Spandana, EBS, SEAP, and XacBank.
15. Brandsma, Judith, and Deena Burjorjee. *Microfinance in the Arab States: Building Inclusive Financial Sectors.* New York: United Nations Capital Development Fund, 2004.
16. Adapted from Cohen, Monique, and Ruth Goodwin-Groen. *Vision and Consistency: US AID Support of Al Amana and the Law on Microfinance in Morocco.* CGAP Donor Good Practices Series, April 2003.

17. Likely improvements to the law include allowing for deposit taking (it presently allows for credit-only services), not allowing the Ministry of Finance to impose interest rate ceilings, and creating a clear law to allow MFIs to transform (without being subject to the same interest rate caps as other commercial banks).

18. Among the sources of sound analysis about ideal regulations and existing approaches are http://www.cgap.org/priorities/enabling_policy_frameworks.html; "Policies, Regulations, and Systems That Promote Sustainable Financial Services to the Poor and Poorest," by Women's World Banking, in *Pathways Out of Poverty (2002);* and *Recommendations for the Creation of a Pro-Microcredit Regulatory Framework,* by Alex Counts and Sharmi Sobhan (2001, revised 2005), which can be downloaded at http://www.gfusa.org/pubdownload/~pubid=7.

19. Zakoura borrowed 11.65 million MAD (about US$1.2 million) during its first three years and 194 million MAD (US$21.9 million) since then from domestic banks including Société Générale Marocaine de Banques, Banque Marocaine du Commerce Extérieur, Banque Centrale Populaire, Banque Européenne d'Investissement, Banque Marocaine du Commerce Intérieur, Crédit du Maroc, Crédit Immobilier et Hotelier, and Caisse Marocaine de Retraite.

20. Gibbons, David, and Jennifer Meehan. "Financing Microfinance for Poverty Reduction," in *Pathways out of Poverty: Innovations in Microfinance for the Poorest Families.* Bloomfield, CT: Kumarian Press, 2002. This influential chapter has informed the investment strategy of many of the newest supporters of microfinance, such as Vinod Khosla, who partnered with Grameen Foundation with an equity investment in Cashpor-India and with Unitus in support of SKS.

21. Edington, Mark. "How to Focus on Breakthrough Organizations When Selecting MFIs." Input paper for the UNCDP/SUM and UNDP Africa. Presented at Global Meeting, May 30–June 1, 2001.

22. Rasmussen estimates that only 40% of microfinance clients in Pakistan are served by profitable MFIs, whereas in Bangladesh that figure is 95%.

23. Bureau of Finance and Economic Development, 2002. This figure is based on a study that took place in 1995, before ACSI was launched, so it may understate the combined coverage of conventional banks and MFIs today.

24. IFAD, *Ethiopia—Rural Financial Intermediation Programme (RUFIP) Formulation Report,* Vols.1–3 (2001).

25. Amha, Wolday. "Managing the Growth of Microfinance Institutions to Reach Large Numbers of Clients: Experience from Ethiopia." Paper presented at Mekele, March 1–2, 2006.

26. The minimum caloric consumption is set by the World Health Organization at 2,200 calories per day. This minimum consumption is estimated in Ethiopia to cost about $10 per month for adults.

27. Bureau of Finance and Economic Development (2003/2004 statistics), 2005.

28. All figures are as of December 2005 unless otherwise stated. This figure for active clients does not include agricultural input loan clients (50,948), which brings total clients to 485,642 as of December 2005.

29. The total number of clients, including agricultural input loan clients (50,948), was 497,573 as of April 2005.

30. Demand estimates calculated in ACSI's 2001–2005 Strategic Plan.

31. Based on active clients, ACSI is meeting approximately 15% of market demand (434,000 [active clients]/2,900,000 [demand] = 15%). However, if one accounts for cumulative clients served, then ACSI has met 30% of market demand (800,000 [clients served]/2,900,000 = 30%).

32. Amhara Regional Cooperative Promotion Bureau, 2004.

33. Amha, Wolday. *Prudential Regulation of the Microfinance Industry: Lessons from Ethiopia.* Association of Ethiopian Microfinance Institutions (AEMFI), Occasional Paper No. 15. Addis Ababa, 2005.

34. CGAP Changemakers. *Reaching More Savers: Episode 1.* http://microfinancegateway. org/resource_centers/savings/changemakers.

35. MicroRate. *Amhara Credit and Savings Institution: Ethiopia.* Report as of August 2005. The full report can be accessed at www.mix.org.

36. Figures for average loan officer caseload include credit clients only. The average caseload per loan officer for credit clients and voluntary savers increased from 209 in 2001 to 530 in 2005.

37. MicroRate, August 2005.

38. Microfinance Information Exchange, *www.mix.org.*

39. Gobezie, Getaneh. *Subsidizing Microcredit Interest: How Important Is It to the Poor?* (2004).

40. Chao-Beroff, Renee, Wolday Amha, Tesfaye Mengesha, Yohanes Sefere, and Kurunde Tesgera. *Enhancing Rural Financial Intermediation in Ethiopia* (2000).

3

Commercialization: Overcoming the Obstacles to Accessing Commercial Funds While Maintaining a Commitment to Reaching the Poorest

Larry Reed

SYNOPSIS

Can money with a commercial price tag be used to reach the world's poorest microfinance clients? This chapter looks at the current supply of commercial capital available for microfinance and compares it with the demand expressed for that capital and the capacity of microfinance institutions to deploy it effectively. It looks closely at the different actors involved in bringing market capital to the grassroots level, so that multi-million-dollar investments can be distributed in $50 and $100 loans. Through interviews with leaders on the supply and demand sides, as well as with those that help build connections between the two, this chapter examines how commercial funds are deployed to serve very poor clients, and the obstacles that prevent this deployment from happening more often. It concludes with recommendations on steps that various actors in the world financial community can take to ensure that funding from domestic and international capital markets is made available to those for whom it will have the most impact.

HAVING OUR CAKE AND EATING IT TOO

These days the left and the right sides of the political spectrum cannot find much on which to agree. Microfinance is one of the exceptions. For liberals, microfinance reaches into the poorest areas of the world, making $50 loans that help people living on the edge of survival move into the economic system by starting their own businesses. For conservatives, microfinance puts the magic of the marketplace to work to help overcome poverty. Microfinance organizations that charge market rates of interest can cover their own costs and expand their operations by borrowing or selling equity and providing commercial returns to investors. By doing this they can attract the almost limitless sources of commercial capital available, reducing the need for public subsidies to take care of the poor.

I have often wondered what would happen if you got the two groups in the same room and had them each describe their reasons for supporting microfinance. How long would it take for them to realize that they were talking about the same thing?

Or are they? The reason microfinance attracts both groups is the illusion that both goals are possible at the same time: you can reach extremely poor people while providing investors with commercial rates of return for their investments. Clearly, there are many microfinance institutions that do reach down to the poorest of the economically active in their countries. There are also many microfinance organizations that make use of commercial funds of different types—savings, borrowings, and equity investments. But are there any institutions that can do both at the same time, reach down to the lowest levels of poverty and pay commercial rates for their funds?

This is currently a key question for our industry. If it is possible to do both at the same time, then one of the major constraints facing microfinance since its inception will suddenly have been lifted. An industry once dependent on subsidies from government donors (which combined ranged from $500 million to $1 billion a year) would now have access to the hundreds of trillions of dollars that are traded every year in the world's capital markets or deposited in savings instruments. On the other hand, if it is not possible to do both at the same time—if you cannot reach the poorest when you have to pay commercial rates on your funds—then the microfinance community is headed for a nasty divide. Those who use commercial funds to fuel their growth will work increasingly with the higher end of the microfinance market. They will generate positive returns by doing this and become an ever-growing presence in their country's financial marketplace, while leaving the poor behind. Those who focus on reaching the very poor will not be able to access commercial funds and will find their growth limited to the subsidies that governments and other donors are willing to provide them.

Some Definitions

One of the challenging aspects of the microfinance field is the lack of precision in some of the terms we use. The title of this chapter contains two terms that are among our industry's most elastic: "commercial funds" and "poorest." I will define what I mean by these terms and some of their close relatives here. My intention is not to establish definitions that will work for everyone, but rather to clarify what these words mean in this chapter.

Commercial Funds

Commercial funds are investment funds that earn a rate of return set in an open market. The cleanest examples are savings deposits from clients who can choose where to deposit their money, and loans made by local financial institutions at a rate that is similar to what they could earn elsewhere in the market. This becomes more complicated with social investment funds or in countries where banks are required to invest a certain percentage of their portfolio in microfinance. The restrictions or regulations placed on these funds can make them available to microfinance institutions (MFIs) at a lower rate than the MFIs might pay for funds in the open market. However, for the purposes of this chapter I am including social investment funds and funds invested to comply with government regulations. Even if they are not purely commercial, these types of funds help move MFIs closer to the commercial market.

Poorest

The Microcredit Summit Campaign (MCS) employs a clear definition of the poorest: those living on less that $1 per day (using purchasing power parity [PPP]) or those living at less than 50% of the national poverty line in their country. Unfortunately, the terms used by MFIs and the data they collect tend to be much less clear than the MCS definition, and for good reason. Measuring incomes can be challenging in parts of the world where accounts are not written down and not all income comes in the form of money. While USAID, SEEP, IRIS, and others work to develop cost-effective tools for the industry to use (see Chapter 1), we are left with very imperfect proxies to assess which organizations are reaching the poorest.

A further complication is the various terms related to poverty that tend to be used interchangeably. Here is my own list detailing how I will use these terms in this chapter:

- *Poorest of the poor:* Those who lack the physical or mental means to produce regular income for themselves and have no one to provide regular income for them. In most cases MFIs cannot reach these clients with credit products, since there is no activity to lend to, although they may be able to reach them with other financial services (and some have come up with creative ways of working with this group).[1]

- *Poorest of the economically active:* The next rung up from the poorest of the poor. These people can earn a living from their own labor but often find themselves unemployed or underemployed, earning less than enough to sustain a livable diet and adequate shelter. They also find themselves vulnerable to economic shocks that take away what little they have earned.

- *Very poor:* Clients with an average outstanding balance of less than $150 or whose average outstanding balance is less than 25% of the per-capita income in their country (as measured by gross national income [GNI] per capita). While this definition relies on imperfect measures, it at least provides a common yardstick for comparing programs.

- *Poor:* All those living below the national poverty line in their respective countries.

An Uncharitably Brief Summary of How We Got Here

The modern microfinance movement began in the early and mid-1970s (though its antecedents go back at least another fifteen centuries to the Buddhist and Hindu temple loan systems in China and India, respectively). In several parts of the world at around the same time unconventional thinkers began to test ways to use finance to harness the innate dignity and creativity of the poor. The chief lesson of these early years was that the poor were good credit risks. With little or no access to capital and a burning drive to improve the lives of their children, the poor demonstrated a willingness to repay their loans in order to maintain access to the potential for a better life.

The next decade brought many refinements in the way in which loans were delivered to the poor and payments were received from them. Lending to groups both large and small became a much more cost-effective way of delivering and collecting loans, and group guarantees became a reliable way of encouraging consistent repayments. Those organizations that drove down transaction costs, maintained high repayment rates, and charged market rates of interest found that they could cover all the costs of their operations. Government money began pouring into the sector, as public donors became intrigued with the concept of a poverty alleviation program that could maintain the value of its assets over time and cover its own costs.

The 1990s became the decade of thinking big. Microfinance institutions that could cover their costs began looking at ways to increase their scale to match the scale of the need in their own countries. But these growing MFIs faced a dilemma: while most of the institutions had started and grown with subsidized funding, there was not enough donor money available to fuel all the growth they sought. So the pioneering microfinance institutions began looking beyond subsidized funds to the marketplace. They began to see that, with their efficient programs, they could afford to pay interest on their capital and still cover their costs. Some decided to become regulated banks so that they could capture domestic savings. Others borrowed from the local commercial sector. Still others reached out to socially conscious international investors and tapped into the investment arm of multilateral organizations such as the International Finance Corporation. Investors became attracted to this market because it afforded them the opportunity to do good while also earning a return on their money. But they faced their own dilemma: With thousands of microfinance organizations out there, most clamoring for more capital, how could they distinguish the good credit risks from the bad? Credit rating agencies sprang up to fill this gap and provide an independent review of the performance of microfinance organizations.

By the turn of the century, the stage was set. Most of the pieces had been assembled to link some of the world's most impoverished people with some of the world's largest sources of capital. What has happened since then? Have we been able to build the bridge that connects the struggling entrepreneur in Ethiopia with the money managers on Wall Street? Better yet, have we been able to connect poor people in one country who want to borrow with poor people in the same country who want to save? Or has the increasing commercialization of the microfinance sector led to a ratcheting up of loan sizes and a move away from serving the very poor?

To answer these questions, I talked with key representatives of four different parts of the microfinance industry: the leaders of retail institutions who reach out to the very poor, raters who evaluate the creditworthiness of microfinance organizations, industry promoters and supporters who seek to build the entire industry, and commercial investors who seek to invest their funds while earning a market rate of return. These people help to form the chain that links commercial funding to the poorest clients.[2]

THE PROFITABILITY OF SERVING THE VERY POOR

What does it take to lend to very poor clients and earn a large enough financial return to attract commercial investments, either from local depositors or from international investors? Table 3.1 uses data from the Microfinance Information Exchange (MIX) Marketplace 2004 Benchmark data. It compares the performance ratios of 302 different microfinance institutions, divided by target market (low end, broad, high end, and small business). The numbers tell an important story about lending to the very poor. Compare those lending at the low end of the market with their cohorts lending to other market segments. They lend much smaller amounts of money (the median outstanding balance is six times lower than for the next segment), work predominantly with women clients (93% vs. 58% and below in the other segments) and operate at high levels of efficiency (with more clients per loan officer and lower costs per loan than the other segments).

This table also illustrates the basic economic equation of lending to the very poor:

- *Lending to the very poor can be profitable.* The median score of those who work at the bottom end of the market shows that they can achieve financial self-sufficiency ratios of greater than 100% and positive returns on equity and assets. (A regression analysis run by the MIX on the data found no statistically significant difference between the returns earned by organizations serving the low end of the market and those serving the upper tiers.)

- *Lending to the very poor costs more.* Despite the fact that the cost per borrower is lower for those lending at the bottom end, their costs as a percentage of their lending portfolio are still significantly higher than those working in other segments.

- *Those that lend to the very poor charge more in interest.* To become profitable these institutions need to charge higher rates of interest to their clients. It costs 31 cents for every dollar in the portfolio for these institutions to lend to the very poor. To cover those costs, they charge enough in interest and fees to earn 34% on their portfolio.[3]

Table 3.1   2004 Microfinance Institutions Benchmarks

	Target Market			
	Low End	Broad	High End	Small Business
Outreach indicators				
Total assets (US$)	2,265,954	8,250,796	3,787,572	16,143,380
Number of active borrowers	14,976	8,239	8,208	5,861
Percentage of women borrowers	93.3	58.7	49.8	48.1
Gross loan portfolio (US$)	1,833,845	5,729,449	13,252,299	11,571,593
Average outstanding balance (US$)	109	754	1,585	1,559
Average outstanding balance/GNI per capita (%)	14.5	51.6	175.3	275.0
Voluntary savings (US$)	—	—	2,513,140	2,291,956
Overall financial performance				
Return on assets (%)	1.2	1.9	4.8	2.0
Return on equity (%)	4.8	7.0	14.5	12.9
Operational self-sufficiency (%)	113	121	127	120
Financial self-sufficiency (%)	104	111	121	115
Revenues				
Financial revenue ratio (%)	31.25	27.4	21.8	22
Profit margin (%)	3.65	10.2	17.4	13.4
Yield on gross portfolio (nominal) (%)	40.2	33.7	23.9	28.2
Yield on gross portfolio (real) (%)	33.7	26.8	21.2	22.1
Expenses				
Total expense ratio (%)	30.9	26.2	16.6	18
Financial expense ratio (%)	5.9	6.35	4.7	3.3
Loan loss provision expense ratio (%)	1	1.45	0.9	1.2
Operating expense ratio (%)	22.65	14.65	11.1	13.8
Personnel expense ratio (%)	12.45	8.35	6.2	6.7
Administrative expense ratio (%)	9.55	6.9	5.3	7.1
Adjustment expense ratio (%)	1.9	1.65	0.8	0.4

(Continued)

Table 3.1   2004 Microfinance Institutions Benchmarks *(Continued)*

	Target Market			
	Low End	Broad	High End	Small Business
Efficiency				
Operating expense/loan portfolio (%)	33	20	14	28
Personnel expense/loan portfolio (%)	18	10	8	12
Average salary/GNI per capita (%)	3	5	10	16
Cost per borrower (US$)	33	144	223	334
Cost per loan (US$)	32	144	223	338
Productivity				
Borrowers per staff member	157	101	71	52
Loans per loan officer	281	204	179	97
Risk				
Portfolio at risk > 30 days (%)	1.5	2.4	2.6	3.4
Loan loss rate (%)	1.1	1.1	0.3	1.6

This is where the discussion between the political left and right begins to break down. How can the poor be empowered, many will ask, when they have to pay higher rates of interest for their loans than the rich? The simple answer is that it costs more to make smaller loans. This should not be surprising. The price per unit of almost every product goes up when it is broken down into small units. Invariably, people who purchase products in smaller units pay more per unit than those who purchase in large quantities. It is the same for money as it is for any other product, the only difference being that when the product is money, the margin charged by the retailer is quoted, whereas for most other products it remains hidden.

In essence, those who access commercial funds and make them available to the very poor act much like the vendors in the poor people's markets. They buy in bulk, break the product down into units small enough for the poor to be able to afford them, and charge enough to cover their costs of packaging and distribution. The figures show that the cost of financing—what microfinance institutions pay for the money they borrow—is a small portion of their overall costs. "The institutions we rate have average operating costs of between 30 and 50 percent," says Damian von Stauffenberg of MicroRate. "Commercial funds cost around 10 percent. Small increases in productivity by the MFI can lower their operating costs enough to totally offset the cost of commercial funds."

THE HUNT

I next looked for individual institutions that met both criteria for this chapter: they provided financial services to the very poor and they accessed commercial funds. What I found was a lot of conflicting statistics and even more strongly conflicting opinions. There are no standard definitions in the industry for terms such as "poorest" and "very poor," and even when those definitions do exist, most MFIs do not track their clients based on those definitions. Some MFIs do a very good job of making sure that their clients are among the poorest in the communities they serve, but the tools they use (e.g., Participatory Wealth Ranking or a poverty index based on land ownership or housing stock) often do not provide data that can be compared across countries.

The data on the MIX Marketplace provide a further illustration of statistics that begin to lose their value when compared across countries. I looked at financially viable organizations with an average loan size of $100 or less. What I found was a list of primarily Asian and African organizations, and one or two Latin American organizations. I then looked for financially viable organizations with an average outstanding balance of less than 25% of the GNI per capita in the country. This resulted in a list that excluded the organizations operating in the poorest countries. I then took an either/or approach and came up with a list of sixteen microfinance organizations that reach very poor clients and use some type of commercial funding to do so (see Table 3.2). This is not an exhaustive list, but it is large enough to show some of the strategies used and the challenges faced by these organizations in using commercial funds to reach the poorest.

This list led to more conflict when I interviewed industry observers. One of the lightning rods for disagreement was my inclusion of Compartamos, a Mexican financial company that lends to the poor primarily through the Village Banking methodology. "I think Compartamos definitely fits this group because they are doing some of the most innovative work in accessing the commercial markets and they reach a large number of very poor clients," said Bob Christen, director of the Boulder Microfinance Training Program. "Their average outstanding balance over GNI per capita is one of the lowest throughout Latin America."

"Compartamos should not be included in this study if you are discussing access to commercial funds for those primarily focused on reaching the poorest," countered Syed Hashemi of the Consultative Group to Assist the Poor (CGAP). "Those that have a primary mandate on working with the poorest may have a different set of problems that they need to deal with. Compartamos is a fantastic organization and does include many very poor clients, but is not focused exclusively on the poorest."

The main point of disagreement here has to do with the focus of the organization. Some institutions focus exclusively on the poorest. They have some sort of means test to verify that their clients meet the poverty threshold of the organization. Other organizations have a broader focus so that they reach those at the bottom end of the economic ladder and those that are one or two rungs above as well.

For this chapter I am looking at organizations that reach the very poor and use commercial funding to do so, whether or not those organizations focus exclusively on the very poor. However, the issue of focus does lead to different strategies and challenges, so I have divided the institutions reviewed into those with an exclusive focus on the very poor and those that have a broader focus and then compared the strategies they employ.

On the funding side I looked at MFIs that paid something close to commercial rates for their funds. In many cases some form of subsidy was still present in the funding the MFIs received, such as the primary lender to the MFI being a government-owned bank set up to serve microfinance lenders (Philippines), or the government mandating that a certain percentage of a commercial bank's assets be allocated to the micro sector (India). Some access funds at commercial rates from local financial institutions, but require subsidized guarantees to do so.

A closer look at Table 3.2 yields some characteristics that these institutions have in common and some differences between them:

- *Different types of legal structures.* Nongovernmental organizations (NGOs), non-bank financial corporations (NBFCs), MFI banks, and commercial banks all made the list.

- *Small average outstanding balances.* Though the size of loans varies by the prosperity of the country, almost all the institutions had very low average outstanding balances, especially compared to the GNI per capita in the country.

- *High costs and high interest rates.* Almost all of the institutions reflected the high costs that go with lending in small amounts and made up for it by charging higher rates of interest. Three exceptions were ACSI (Ethiopia), Kashf (Pakistan), and Nirdhan (Nepal), which were able to pay very low salaries to their employees (in comparison with the other MFIs on this list) and pass these savings on to their clients by charging much lower rates of interest.

- *Large client bases.* All have more than 25,000 clients, and Compartamos, the largest on the list, has over 400,000 clients.

Table 3.2 Microfinance Institutions That Serve the Very Poor and Use Commercial Funding

Name of Organization	Country	Type of Organization	Total Clients	Avg. Out. Bal.	Avg Bal./GNI per cap	Gross Loan Portfolio	Return on Assets	Return on Equity	OSS	PAR (30)	Fin'l Revenue Ratio	Total Expense Ratio	Fin'l Expense Ratio	Op. Expense Ratio	Cost per Borrower
Exclusive focus															
ACSI	Ethiopia	NBFC	351,163	$104	94.30%	$36,414,559	7.54%	19.45%	231.79%	1.75%	13.26%	5.72%	1.74%	4.25%	5.9
CRECER	Bolivia	Other	55,617	$161	16.70%	$8,933,065	8.46%	19.90%	129.86%	0.41%	36.78%	28.32%	4.93%	22.99%	50.0
ProMujer	Bolivia	NGO	48,496	$117	15.40%	$7,150,439	7.09%	10.78%	140.78%	0.81%	24.47%	17.38%	1.52%	14.87%	32.5
SHARE	India	NBFC	368,996	$109	15.40%	$40,218,274	3.15%	24.63%	120.03%	0.19%	29.77%	24.81%	10.59%	14.22%	17.1
Spandana	India	NBFC	385,996	$142	14.90%	$54,621,671	8.35%	94.10%	192.55%	0.01%	17.91%	9.30%	5.35%	3.68%	5.5
Nirdhan	Nepal	Bank	68,601	$110	42.20%	$3,587,302	-0.02%	-0.70%	101.15%	10.30%	14.09%	11.41%	3.87%	6.50%	14.0
LAPO	Nigeria	NGO	29,812	$63	16.20%	$1,194,633	8.86%	15.95%	125.22%	1.00%	44.01%	35.15%	1.25%	31.25%	28.1
KMBI	Philippines	NGO	80,078	$52	4.40%	$4,129,804	5.83%	18.00%	113.60%	0.20%	48.72%	42.89%	3.37%	39.34%	29.9
TSKI	Philippines	NGO/Rural bank	162,867	$70	3.60%	$11,362,079	4.31%	44.35%	114.17%	1.49%	34.75%	30.43%	4.49%	24.35%	29.8
TSPI	Philippines	NGO	144,064	$131	6.80%	$9,153,101	10.87%	28.61%	120.58%	0.87%	41.35%	34.29%	2.64%	29.78%	33.7
Small Enterprise Foundation	South Africa	NGO	27,538	$146	3.90%	$4,024,662	-4.42%	-9.84%	91.94%	0.49%	50.42%	54.84%	5.09%	49.44%	90.1
Broad focus															
Banco Nordeste (CrediAmigo)	Brazil	Bank Division	162,868	$250	8.10%	$40,749,313	4.31%	38.01%	110.02%	1.88%	47.30%	42.99%	16.15%	23.86%	56.9
OISASL/Sinapi Aba	Ghana	S&L/NGO	53,029	$80	21.00%	$4,240,557	0.49%	0.73%	103.38%	1.01%	40.00%	38.69%	0.90%	37.62%	50.1
Compartamos	Mexico	NBFC	402,007	$326	4.80%	$101,023,790	18.26%	48.50%	167.88%	0.56%	69.75%	41.55%	9.84%	30.07%	121.4
Zakoura	Morocco	NGO	174,480	$144	9.50%	$24,280,795	13.85%	26.53%	166.05%	0.46%	34.81%	20.97%	2.31%	20.59%	26.3
Kashf	Pakistan	NGO	67,552	$119	0.40%	$8,068,304	8.97%	17.53%	186.97%	0.66%	19.27%	10.31%	2.02%	7.74%	17.0

All data from the Marketplace MIX Year End 2004

These institutions pursue different routes to access commercial funds. Here are the main strategies they employed:

- *Linking a commercial bank with NGOs and self-help groups.* SHARE and Spandana in India both receive most of their funding from ICICI Bank, the largest private bank in India. ICICI reaches the very poor through partnerships with grassroots MFIs. One method for doing this is by using the NGO or NBFC as an agent for disbursing and collecting loans while ICICI provides the capital. Another is by securitizing portfolios, buying the loan book from the MFI at an agreed-upon rate, and thus freeing up capital for the MFI to lend to new clients. Last year ICICI Bank concluded a $4.3 million securitization deal with SHARE, which included assistance from Grameen Foundation USA. ICICI bank currently has partnership arrangements with over 100 MFIs in India that combined provide $300 million in credit to over 3 million clients. ICICI categorizes 20% of these clients as "very poor" and 92% as living on $2 per day or less.

- *Going down market.* Banco do Nordeste, a development bank in the northeast of Brazil, developed a credit program for reaching microentrpreneurs with support from ACCION International. Using the bank's existing deposit base, CrediAmigo built a $40 million portfolio serving over 160,000 clients in just five years. CrediAmigo has been able to piggyback on the bank's existing branch infrastructure while also developing some of its own outlets. It now has 166 agencies in eleven northeast states of Brazil, the poorest section of the country. Banco do Nordeste has also developed innovative ways of providing financial services in remote areas of the country using point-of-sale devices in local grocery stores.[4]

- *Playing in the big leagues.* With over 400,000 clients Compartamos is one of the largest MFIs in Latin America. To support its growth Compartamos has moved beyond the credit lines it established with commercial banks to selling bonds to institutional investors in Mexico. Its bonds, issued by Citibank/Banamex, received an AA rating from Standard & Poor's and Fitch. These bonds have become so popular in the Mexican financial markets that the last round of $30 million was oversubscribed almost 3 to 1. All told, Comparatamos has raised over $70 million with these bonds.

- *Local borrowing.* Lift Above Poverty Organization (LAPO) in Nigeria funds over one-third of its portfolio with loans from local banks. The

Small Enterprise Foundation (SEF) in South Africa has as its largest investor a social investment fund established in that country. TSKI in the Philippines supports most of its portfolio with financing from the People's Credit and Finance Corporation, a government-created vehicle for investing in MFIs.

- *Local borrowing with international loan guarantees.* OISASL in Ghana borrows from a commercial bank there, but the commercial bank required a guarantee from the Opportunity International Loan Guarantee Fund to establish the relationship. SEF has a similar guarantee from Shared Interest.

- *Borrowing from foreign sources.* Most of KMBI's funding comes from Oikocredit, a Dutch social investment company that lends to KMBI in local currency. SEF borrows from Triodos Bank in the Netherlands, with foreign currency cover provided by HIVOS, a Dutch NGO.

- *Mobilizing deposits.* The Opportunity International Bank of Malawi (OIBM) did not make the cut for institutions to be included in the table because of its 86% operational self-sustainability. That is in part because it is a young and growing institution, and also because its primary source of loan capital has high administrative expenses—the deposits of the poor. Using smart cards that store fingerprint images to identify clients, OIBM has established over 45,000 savings accounts for poor clients in three years, with total deposits of over $5 million and an average deposit balance of $119. It finds greater demand for savings facilities in poor communities than credit, with five savers for every borrower.

Serving the Very Poor Alongside the Not as Poor

Those organizations that serve the very poor as a part of their client base, but not exclusively, have an advantage in generating the revenues needed to pay for commercial sources of funds. They have a larger market to work with in any given community and will have larger average loan sizes than organizations working only with the very poor. The question is whether the very poor will remain a part of their client base as they grow, or whether the built-in incentives of a financial institution will cause them to move toward less-poor clients. Has utilizing commercial funds caused these organizations to move away from the lowest end of the market? The leaders of these organizations don't think so. Benjie Montemayor of OISASL puts it most clearly: "If you're serious about outreach to the poor you must be serious about commercial borrowing. Everything else is a myth."

Carlos Labarthe of Compartamos agrees with Montemayor: "As we grow we are continuing with the same client group that we started with. It is the one that gives us life. It is our roots and our soul."

Both of these CEOs warn against using average loan size as a primary measure of whether or not an organization is moving away from its mission. "If we are doing our job well, our average loan size should be going up. We have many clients that have been with us for 15 years. They have been very successful and their credit needs have grown along with our businesses. We have had to develop new products to support them," says Labarthe.

Montemayor sees a growing average loan size as a sign that OISASL is achieving its mission of transformation in the lives of its clients. "Maintaining a low average loan size is an indication of a high dropout rate," says Montemayor. "Over 30 percent of our clients are in their fifth loan cycle and above. We want to keep growing with these clients. If that makes our average loan size go up, that is good. We want to make sure our average first loan size stays small, but we want to see clients growing beyond that level."

Damian von Stauffenberg of MicroRate compares this type of increase in average loan size to gravity, a natural phenomenon that occurs as clients' businesses grow. "The best organizations I have seen know who their target market is and stick with it," he says. "They know at what level a client should enter the program and at what level a client should leave." (See Chapter 1 for a discussion by Van Bastelaer and Zeller on the difficulties of using loan size as an indicator of the poverty level of clients.)

But as they grow, what prevents these institutions from moving primarily to higher-end customers? Labarthe points to two key factors for Compartamos. First, their primary lending methodology is Village Banks, a methodology with proven attraction for the very poor. Second is the way that they choose communities to move into. "Mexico has 2,544 municipalities and the government divides them in four categories according to their level of poverty—very high, high, medium, and low," Labarthe says. "Forty-six percent of our clients live in municipalities with high or very high levels of poverty. Our Board of Directors tracks this indicator every month."

Montemayor agrees that the core methodology should help ensure that the program attracts the very poor, but he also points out that adding deposit services eventually leads to a broadening of the client base. "We want to provide savings services because we know that this is a service that is needed by the very poor," he says. "The infrastructure to set up deposit services is very expensive. So we want to attract savings deposits from everyone, not just from the very poor. But if we want to attract the deposits of higher-end customers, we are going to have to be able to provide them with other financial services as well. Otherwise we will lose out to the other financial institutions that can provide them a whole range of credit and payment services."

Necessary Preconditions

Montemayor describes ten preconditions for an MFI to access commercial funds:

- Readily available financial performance information
- Ability to apply best practices
- Good governance and management that focuses on profitability and results
- Very low portfolio at risk (PAR)
- Appropriate provisioning and write-off policies
- Strong performance trend
- Products priced to cover full costs
- Rating by professional raters
- Strong and visionary leaders
- An environment conducive to microfinance

Labarthe emphasizes transparency in dealing with the financial markets. "People working in the financial markets consider the microfinance sector very strange. They don't know if they can trust our numbers. We have to be transparent in the numbers we provide and the way we govern our institutions. When we do this we support the whole sector because banks will see this as a good place to invest their money." No surprise, then, that Compartamos was one of the first winners of the CGAP Financial Transparency Award.

Both Montemayor and Labarthe talked about the difficulty of convincing a bank to lend to them the first time. Compartamos's first line of credit required a government guarantee, a 30% liquidity guarantee, and the backing of the full credit portfolio. Even with all that backing, Carlos still had to take the bank officials out to visit clients and demonstrate to them how the program worked. Benjie had it a little easier, but OISASL's first loan from a local bank required a 50% guarantee from Opportunity International's Loan Guarantee Fund. Once they established these relationships, though, the banks gained more confidence in lending to MFIs. OISASL's most recent loan required a guarantee of only 20%. Compartamos's current lines of credit and most recent bond issue have much better conditions now and in some cases do not require any type of guarantee.

This points to one of the chief advantages of being able to utilize commercial funds while lending to the very poor. Once an MFI demonstrates its creditworthiness to the market, it can continue growing by obtaining more investments. Good performance feeds on itself, making more capital available to lend to more clients, which provide more income to the MFI. The MFI can use this to expand to new areas and/or develop a wider range of products for its clients.

Additional Challenges That Come with an Exclusive Focus

Of course, the preconditions supplied by Montemayor and Labarthe apply to any MFI, regardless of the type of client it tries to reach. Those who seek to serve the very poor as their primary client base face additional challenges in making the financial equation of serving the very poor work for them. Because of the higher unit cost involved in breaking loans down into smaller amounts, these MFIs have to find ways to lower costs or increase income sufficiently to pay their operating costs and the cost of capital. Here are some of the key strategies they used to accomplish this:

- *Massive scale with heavy regimentation.* Many of the institutions that exclusively serve the very poor do so with a very structured and regimented branch replication model. They have the manuals, procedures, operating systems, staff training programs, daily schedules, and recruitment techniques needed to get new lending branches established and profitable in less than a year. Once they have this in place, they can continue establishing new branches until they have enough scale to pay for their overhead and the cost of capital. With their relationship with ICICI Bank, SHARE and Spandana are able to focus on what they do best—establish and maintain customer relationships among the very poor, deliver loans, and collect repayments—while ICICI Bank provides the capital they need to grow. Since ICICI provides its funds through either an agency arrangement or securitization, the amount of capital that SHARE and Spandana receive is not limited by the amount of equity they have on their balance sheets. This massive scale approach works best in environments with high population density among the very poor.

- *Start with the very poor, then expand the client group.* John De Wit of the Small Enterprise Foundation (SEF) works in rural South Africa, an area that does not have high population density and that requires high salaries to attract educated people as employees, giving him the highest operating expense ratio of any of the MFIs listed in Table 3.2. John does not think that the Compartamos strategy of serving a broad market from the start would work in his context.

We found that the poorest were not comfortable in a program that also included people who were less poor. So we started with a participatory wealth ranking system and only allowed in people who were earning less than half of the poverty line. After we have been operating in the community for four years we do away with the cutoff line and allow anyone to participate. We weren't sure what the impact would be on the very poor to have less poor clients in the program. Our research shows that that there is no negative impact and there could be some positive effect from having successful business people in the center meetings. Of course, by this time the poorer clients we started with have grown their businesses and gained more confidence in running them.

- *Establish long-term relationships with customers.* In providing financial services to the very poor, an MFI spends a lot of money to acquire and train clients. The cost of maintaining clients after that is relatively low in comparison. MFIs can increase their income if they maintain the client relationship longer, can sell more services to their clients, and can help their clients' businesses grow so that they need larger loans and more services. This is the strategy being pursued in the Philippines by Rose Castro of KMBI and Angel De Leon of TSKI. According to Castro,

We see the need for vertical expansion as well as expansion in numbers. We need to reach lower to the ultra-poor and higher with growing clients. We support community development efforts that help stimulate business activity in poor communities and we provide business development services for our existing clients. We've started a club that teaches entrepreneurship to those with growing businesses. We also sell life insurance to our clients that covers them and their family members. This provides a needed service to them, makes our loans less risky, earns us income and provides us with a competitive advantage in the marketplace. Now the other MFIs are providing insurance as well, and they've set the terms to match what we're providing.

- So does she mind having to compete to reach poor people? "No, competition is healthy, as long as it is done ethically. We've had to improve our services and our performance in order to stay competitive. In the end it's the clients who benefit, and retaining customers benefits the organization in the long run," Castro states.

In another section of the same country Angel de Leon of TSKI has a similar strategy. "We are creating community-based enterprises for communities that are too poor to support our regular group lending program," he says, "and we are offering individual loans to the entrepreneurs who are growing out of our group lending program. We are also offering training and business development services to help them grow their businesses. Without that we found that the loan sizes started to level off. The poor don't need constantly increasing loan sizes unless their businesses are growing."

And how does he pay for providing the business development services? "We charge the clients for them and then provide them with loans to pay those charges," de Leon says. "TSKI earns money in providing the service and then earns again when the client applies what she has learned and needs to take out a larger loan for her growing business."

BLENDED STRATEGIES

Providing commercial funding to the very poor requires the mobilization of savings and deposits, the establishment and maintenance of relationships with customers among the very poor, the ability to break large sums of money down into small units and then collect repayments, and the infrastructure needed to provide a place for staff to work from, clients to meet, and data to be stored. The realization that not all of these activities need to be housed in the same institution is fueling much of the current wave of innovation in the industry. The work of ICICI Bank in India provides a good example of this: the bank handles the work of deposit mobilization and treasury management while NGOs do the work of employing low-cost mechanisms to build and maintain customer relationships. Some of the other strategies that unite the work of two or more institutions to deliver services to the very poor include

- *Piggybacking on existing infrastructure.* The expense of setting up branch offices in new locations forms another large component of costs for many MFIs. Rather than incurring this expense, some MFIs are finding ways to deliver financial services to the poor through existing retail stores, post offices, or even marketplace vendors. This is the approach being employed by Banco do Nordeste in Brazil as it expands its financial services into the remote regions of the Amazon valley. By setting up point-of-sale devices in rural grocery stores and hooking them into the bank through the phone network, the bank is able to offer financial services in areas where it could not afford to build offices or employ staff.

- *Piggybacking on existing networks.* A lot of the recent growth in microfinance in India has come with NGOs and banks using the established infrastructure of self-help groups (SHGs) to deliver their financial services. A recent study estimates that over 6 million clients in India receive access to microfinance services through SHGs.[5] In other parts of the world MFIs work through established community groups and savings clubs.

- *Linking financial services with retailers that serve the very poor.* Retail operations that work in poor communities have begun to see how they might move into providing financial services as well as a way of building the economies in the communities where they work and increasing sales at their stores. Carlos Labarthe reported that at the same time the Central Bank issued a banking license for Compartamos they also issued one for Electra, a large department store chain in Mexico. In the Philippines the Shoemart chain of companies also owns Banco de Oro, which is now looking at providing microfinancial services in some of the poor communities where it operates.

- *Uniting NGO and bank operations.* Several of the banking institutions in Table 3.1 also operate NGOs that serve the same client base. The NGO and the bank work hand in glove to support the common overall mission of transforming the lives of the clients and their communities. The NGOs play several different roles in conjunction with the bank. LAPO in Nigeria and OISASL in Ghana have NGOs that provide business development services and HIV/AIDS training to the clients of the bank. In the Philippines TSKI sells its profitable branches to K Bank, a thrift bank that has basically the same board and management team as TSKI. In this way the bank brings in only branches that are profitable and pays for the branches out of the profits that the branch generates. This helps the bank to remain profitable as it expands. CARD Bank and CARD NGO in the Philippines operate in a similar manner.

- *Driving down transaction costs with technology.* A study in South Africa found that a financial transaction that takes place in a bank branch with a teller costs $1.25 to process. The same transaction at an ATM costs $0.30, and one done over a cell phone costs $0.08. Many commercial banks and MFIs working with the very poor are looking at ways to use technology to lower their transaction costs, enabling them to reach even poorer clients. This way they can focus human interaction in the areas where it is most needed while letting technology handle routine transactions. One example of an MFI using technology combined with the preceding two strategies is the work being done by OIBM to reach rural farmers. OIBM has developed a loan product to farmers organized by the Small Holders Association in Malawi. The loan is disbursed on a smart card, which the farmers use at point-of-sale devices placed in farm stores. The loan is guaranteed by the grain marketing company, which pays off the loan when the farmer brings in the crop. Traditionally, loans to farmers have been too risky for MFIs in a country where rainfall is not consistent from year to year. Working on a contract with the World Bank, Opportunity International developed a crop insurance based on the rainfall index that is provided in conjunction with the loan. Satellite images are used for verification, and if the rainfall does not meet necessary levels, the farmer's loan is paid off by the insurance.

WELL-MEANING MONEY IN SEARCH OF GOOD INVESTMENTS

By applying global best practices, adapting them to local conditions, and throwing in a lot of creativity, several MFIs have found ways to reach the poorest while borrowing from commercial sources. But what about the other side of the equation? Who is investing in microfinance operations, and what motivates their investments?

Microfinance has found new suitors. Once the darling of government aid programs, it now gets much more attention from the global financial community. Pierre Omidyar, the founder of eBay, along with his wife, Pam, recently donated $100 million to Tufts University with a unique condition: the money had to be invested by Tufts in international microfinance activities. Tufts expects this microfinance fund to earn returns similar to those from its other investment portfolios.[6]

The Consultative Group to Assist the Poor (CGAP), a World Bank–sponsored network of institutions supporting microfinance, estimates that foreign capital investment in this field reached US$2 billion at the end of 2005 and is growing at 20% a year. CGAP also notes that most of these funds are concentrated in a small number of leading microfinance institutions and in two regions of the world: Latin America and Eastern Europe.[7]

A recent issue of the *MicroBanking Bulletin*, an industry trade publication loaded with comparative statistics, lists over fifty microfinance funds. You can find them domiciled in the same locations as other international investment funds: Luxembourg, Switzerland, the Cayman Islands, Mauritius, Netherlands, Panama, and the United States. Some are offshoots of government organizations such as the International Finance Corporation or USAID, while others are purely private affairs, such as the Calvert Foundation.[8]

Looking through the websites and literature of these funds, you find a common emphasis on "doing well by doing good." The funds stress the power of the marketplace to lift people out of poverty while at the same time generating competitive returns for their investors. Yet while they emphasize the marketplace discipline of their funds, the people who started and lead these funds all have a strong sense of mission.

Bob Pattillo represents this group well. A successful entrepreneur in the family real estate business, he realized that he could have more impact by putting his financial skills to work now on issues of global poverty rather than waiting to amass a large fortune and give it away at the end of his life. He created Gray Ghost, a microfinance "fund of funds" that invests in a portfolio of microfinance funds. Pattillo uses his entrepreneurial background to look for strategic opportunities in the microfinance market. He uses this fund-of-funds approach to provide exit vehicles for microfinance investors. He also created an emergency liquidity fund to help MFIs maintain a constant supply of capital to their clients while they are waiting for new rounds of longer-term financing.

Pattillo celebrates the "double bottom line" approach he and the other investors take to this work. "What we are doing is as important for the investor as it is for the micro-entrepreneur that gets the loan," he says. "This is a sustainable international investment vehicle that feeds the soul."

Yet Pattillo finds that the funds he invests in face a common problem: more investment funds available than good places to invest the money. He cites several reasons for this:

- Public- and private-sector funds all competing to invest money in a small number of large-scale and profitable microfinance institutions

- Microfinance organizations wary about letting in new equity investors for fear of losing their mission to serve the poor

- An industry that is still squeamish about too much leverage

- Foreign exchange risk exposure when most funds lend in hard currency while the MFIs that receive their investments lend in their local currencies

Since this is a relatively new field, most microfinance funds are very young. The industry has not yet developed disclosure standards or benchmarks for performance of microfinance funds (something CGAP has begun to work on). And while the fund managers speak often of their social mission, most cannot say whether the organizations they invest in really reach the very poor, or whether the returns their funds require limit them to serving only the safest and most profitable microfinance institutions.

Pattillo has been fiddling with instruments to keep his fund focused as clearly on its social bottom line as it is on the financial one. He has developed a Social Return on Investment index that gives high scores to MFIs that link their financing with other development activities in the same communities, serve hard-to-reach populations, or develop innovations in serving a wider range of client needs. His hope is that many funds can adopt a similar form of social return index and compare results.

Steve Hardgrave is another player on the funding side of the equation. After earning his MBA at Berkeley, Hardgrave took off to Chiapas, Mexico, where he helped found a microfinance organization. Now he works as an investment manager for the Omidyar Network, helping to invest the network's money in programs that support self-empowerment.

Hardgrave explains how the Omidyar Network's approach is different from that of Gray Ghost: "We don't give any special advantage for those organizations that serve the very poor. "We don't go down the double bottom line. Our mission is even harder to quantify. We ask, 'Does this institution promote self-empowerment among an underserved market?' With this standard we are as happy to invest in both the high and the low end of the microfinance markets."

The Omidyar Network has both a foundation arm that gives grants and an investment arm that expects a commercial return. "We use our nonprofit donations more for public goods, supporting the industry as a whole," Hardgrave says. Omidyar has supported the development of favorable regulations, information exchanges, rating agencies, credit bureaus, and low-cost technology for recording transactions. In this way they seek to make the microfinance market more accessible to the commercial sector.

"Our theory on microfinance is that, if you can scale these things up and do so commercially, then capital is no longer a problem. This should free up capital from the international financial institutions to go down market to those MFIs that really need it," explains Hardgrave.

BRIDGING THE INFORMATION GAP

For an investor trying to support MFIs the high cost of locating the good performers and then conducting due diligence often stands in the way of making investments in more institutions. It is much less costly to follow someone else's lead and invest in an MFI where someone has already done the research.

Into this gap have come rating agencies—independent third parties that have developed tools for assessing the performance of a microfinance institution and can give an unbiased opinion on its health.

Damian von Stauffenberg was working with the International Finance Corporation when he noticed the need to rate MFIs. He left to start up MicroRate, the first rating agency focused on microfinance. MicroRate focuses on Latin America and Africa. In 2005 it conducted fifty-three ratings and have plans to do sixty in 2006. "Demand for the ratings has picked up since commercial funds have become available," says von Stauffenberg. "MFIs know that they need to get rated if they want to get noticed by the commercial investors. Many investment funds require an independent rating before they will start discussions."

A rating costs about $10,000. In the first years they were paid mostly by donors through such funds as the CGAP rating fund. Now von Stauffenberg says that he is seeing more and more MFIs paying for their ratings out of their own retained earnings.

From his vantage point reviewing ratings of many different sizes and types of MFIs in Latin America and Africa, von Stauffenberg has an interesting perspective on the industry. He finds the move to commercial sources of funds to be a positive trend in the industry, one that promotes efficiency and improves customer service. What about mission drift when an organization has to pay commercial rates for its capital? "I've seen it happen," says von Stauffenberg, "but what I see more often is a mission U-turn. MFIs start using commercial funds and think they have to move upmarket to get more income and cover their costs. When they go there they find the market to be very competitive and very different from the one they know. They lose money very quickly and soon come running back to the market they know best."

And why is there more social investment funding available than there are places to put it? "The problem is absorptive capacity," says von Stauffenberg. "Most MFIs are too small to make effective use of the funds, and those that are large usually have lots of money available locally." He goes on to cite the lack of good foreign exchange cover as a factor limiting the number of institutions that can use foreign investments.

Aldo Moauro serves as the director of Microfinanza Rating, a rating firm spun off from Microfinanza srl, a consulting company specializing in micro and rural finance based in Milan, Italy. Microfinanza Rating has conducted over 100 ratings in twenty-five countries. The cost of these ratings ranges from $10,000 to $15,000, depending on the size of the institution.

Microfinanza Rating offers four types of rating products. First is a mini-rating for smaller institutions to help them prepare for a more formal rating. Next is a private rating, where an institution can see how it scores without the rating being made public, giving the institution an early indicator of where it needs to change in order to improve its score. Third is the public rating, where the final rating document is disclosed to the financial community through publication on the CGAP website. Their fourth product is a social rating that looks at the mission of an MFI, the poverty level of its clients, and the impact of its services.

The primary function of these ratings is to help the institutions being rated gain access to investment funds. "We feel like we can really help MFIs to access financial markets and commercial sources of funds," says Moauro. "Our credibility is very good with investors, and some investors require an independent rating before they will make an investment."

Right now he does not see investors paying much attention to the level of poverty reached by the institutions they invest in. "Investing in microfinance is the social issue for them," he says. "They are not interested in exploring much further."

However, he believes that this will not always be the case. "We see a time when a good social rating will be a competitive advantage for an MFI," Moauro says, "both internally and externally. It is important for an institution to be able to show to its staff, management and board that it is achieving good social performance. This will help it retain staff who are committed to its mission. And a good social rating will also be a way that a microfinance organization can promote itself to social investors."

Another leading rating agency, Micro Credit Ratings International Limited (MCRIL), hails from India. This agency has conducted over 350 ratings worldwide, most of them in Asia. Sanjay Gandhi of MCRIL says, "Our ratings provide two things to the MFI: better access to capital and a review of strengths and weaknesses that they can use to improve their organization."

Like Microfinanza, MCRIL is developing a social rating product. "We discovered that investors also desire to know the MFI's impact on the social front, so we designed a new product called the 'social rating' which reviews what an MFI's impact is on the poor. This tool has taken off and found good acceptance in the market," says Gandhi.

All three rating agencies recognize that their role still requires subsidy. CGAP and the InterAmerican Development Bank created a rating fund that approves rating agencies and pays a portion of the cost of conducting a rating. MCRIL also conducts a lot of ratings for the Small Industrial Development Bank in India (SIDBI), which pays them directly for the service.

"We know that CGAP will be exiting in a couple of years," says Moauro. "It is very important for us to reduce costs and become more efficient so that MFIs can afford our service."

BUILDING THE INFRASTRUCTURE

The role of CGAP in establishing the rating fund serves as an example of its key role in building the microfinance industry and helping microfinance organizations access the commercial market. Built as a consortium of donor organizations supporting microfinance, and sponsored by the World Bank, CGAP has been the catalyst in a host of industry support services and innovations, including the Pro Poor Innovation Challenge, the Transparency Awards, the Microfinance Information Exchange Marketplace (MIX), donor best-practices guidelines, the MicroFinance Management Institute, and the MicroFinance Gateway on the Internet. Through this work CGAP seeks to help build the infrastructure to support a financial industry where all poor people have access to the financial services they need.

Elizabeth Littlefield became the CEO of CGAP after working on Wall Street as an investment banker. This gives her a unique perspective on the industry. "I think there is too much of an emphasis on Wall Street and not enough emphasis on Main Street," she says. "The Wall Street solutions are only temporary. We are doing development work and the object of development is to help countries build permanent self-sustaining local markets, markets that recycle the vast savings that are outside the system into productive loans." She points out that in most of the countries where MFIs work the poor do not have access to safe places to save their money, and that this is often the first service desired by the poorest clients. "In fact, we find that most poor households are net savers. Most MFIs that evolve to become licensed to take deposits, find themselves flooded with liquidity. Injecting cash from the North to the South is necessary in some cases in the short run. But in most cases liquidity is not the problem; institutional intermediation capacity is the bottleneck."

Bob Christen also finds all the discussion about international social investment funds rather irrelevant to the big picture. "Though social investment funds represent an important transitory step in the evolution of the industry, they're a rather expensive way to move money around," he says. "The ultimate solution is working with the banks that already have the money. You've got to work with the banks. In the long run that's the only way to provide the broad range of services needed by the poor."

Christen has been around the microfinance industry for more than 20 years, starting with ACCION International and then working as an independent consultant, then with CGAP, and now with the Boulder Microfinance Institute (a training program he started). He is the main force behind several key support services in the microfinance industry, including the *MicroBanking Bulletin* and MIX.

The difficulty with the big bank approach, Bob acknowledges, is that banks are very slow at innovation. "Banks will only do what they see being done comfortably by other banks in their country. When it comes to real product innovation, banks copy NGOs, mostly by hiring away their staff."

What's more, the lower down the economic ladder you go, the longer it will take to get banks involved. "Banks don't want their lobbies filled with poor people," he says. "But beyond the culture clash, there is the problem of interest rates. Serving the poor involves higher costs, which need to be paid for with higher interest rates, rates at levels that often make banks feel uncomfortable."

Francis Pelekamoyo has seen this issue from both sides. He is a former governor of the Central Bank of Malawi and now serves as the board chair of OIBM in Malawi. He points to the differences in culture between microfinance banks and commercial banks that try to go downmarket. "Serving the poor is a part of our culture. Our clients feel so relaxed here. They are not lectured at, but welcomed with open arms. One of the commercial banks in town tried to copy our approach. They dropped the minimum balance for their savings accounts. People flooded the bank, but they were not their type of clients; they were our type of clients. The banking hall became so full that their regular clients stopped coming. The bank responded by charging high teller fees for those with small balances, and the poor people stopped coming."

Pelekamoyo thinks that one of the primary assets of microfinance institutions is its focus on developing a staff that shows respect to those who have not had access to financial services before. "One of our achievements is that we have brought banking to a group of Malawians that had no knowledge of banking at all. Other banks don't have the patience for this."

So how do we bridge this gap between institutions that have capital available but lack the tools and the will to make it available to the people who most need it and could make the best use of it? Christen suggests two strategies. In poorer countries like Malawi he thinks it is more likely for the gap to be filled by NGOs converting themselves into banks and providing the wide range of financial services needed by the poor. This may serve as the example needed to attract other banks into the market. In countries with more developed financial markets he thinks it is more likely that an existing bank will respond to competitive pressure by trying to open up a new market segment that serves the very poor. "This requires finding bank owners that are committed to reaching this segment, but when you do you have all the resources of the bank available to serve this market," says Christen. "Those who do this find that it improves the operations of the whole bank as the notions of customer service and efficiency present in the micro sector begin to permeate the whole bank."

OBSTACLES TO GROWTH

So far we have heard from the leaders of MFIs and banks that use commercial funds to serve the very poor, the managers of funds that invest in these institutions, the raters that provide the marketplace with the information it needs to make investments, and the industry supporters that supply the research and training needed to grow the industry. If all of these different players can work together to make it possible for commercial funds to reach the very poor, what prevents this from happening more often? What precludes the industry from scaling to match the number of very poor people who could make productive use of these services? The leaders of the MFIs point to several obstacles they have faced in obtaining access to commercial funds for lending to the very poor:

- *Lack of trained people.* Leaders of profitable MFIs consistently list human capital as a more serious constraint on their growth than financial capital. Once they demonstrate to the financial markets that they are a good credit risk, they have access to more financial capital than they can deploy. But they do not have access to readily available personnel trained in delivering services to the very poor. Usually they are very particular about the people they hire, wanting to make sure that they bring in people who share their mission and values and who will treat their clients with respect and dignity. This requires investing in regular training programs not only for new employees but for existing employees as well, all of which take time and money.

- *Costly information systems.* Large-scale operations utilizing client deposits and borrowed funds from a variety of sources need robust information systems that give confidence to investors and regulators that the money is being managed well. For those organizations that started as NGOs and have become finance companies or banks, this is a constant challenge, since the way they operate does not seem to fit the way that most banking software is written. Although more programs are being developed for microfinance institutions, most do not yet have a sufficient base of users to sustain the level of technical support needed to keep these programs operating well.

- *Foreign exchange risk.* Most of the social investment funds lend only in hard currency. In many countries with the poorest clients there are no adequate means available for hedging foreign exchange risk. This means that this source of funds may be cut off from those areas that need them most.

- *Competition from subsidized sources.* Godwin Ehigiamousoe of LAPO described the initial challenge he faced in gaining the confidence of both clients and banks because of subsidized lending programs run by the government that did not enforce credit discipline and did not get their money paid back. In other countries government-run programs for lending money to MFIs may be crowding out private sector lenders and providing a disincentive for MFIs to develop deposit services for their clients.

- *High transaction costs.* With the exception of places like India and Ethiopia, where MFIs can pay very little and still retain high-quality staff, lending to the very poor entails high transaction costs. MFIs compensate for this by charging high interest rates. But what happens to the MFI that wants to work in remote areas where the local economies may not be able to support high interest rates? This is the challenge faced by SEF in South Africa. The national economy pushes up the price for talented people. Recent bad experiences with consumer credit have caused the government to look askance at any organization charging high interest rates. And the rural areas where SEF works do not have the same level of economic activity that is occurring in the urban areas. Here the challenge is to find ways to lower transaction costs to a level where the interest rate paid by the clients can cover the cost of delivering the service while remaining affordable to the client.

- *Constraining regulation.* Regulation put in place to protect the savings deposits of the middle class may impede the rapid expansion of financial services to the poor. Minimum capitalization requirements, reserve ratios based on collateral, expensive infrastructure obligations, and branch-by-branch approval of bank expansion can create barriers to entry and to expansion that slow the growth of those that serve the very poor. As we have seen, serving the very poor with commercial funding often requires large-scale operations. Regulations that slow the expansion of banks focused on the very poor, or that require large reserves on the unsecured lending portfolio, may make it impossible for formal financial institutions to serve this market profitably. In addition, the advent of new technologies is making old concepts of branch locations and cash handling obsolete, and central banks are having a hard time keeping up.

WHAT SHOULD BE DONE?

1. Break the logjam by creating competition to go downmarket. As long as investors in MFIs view all microfinance operations the same, regardless of the client base they serve or the impact they achieve, there will continue to be a large amount of investment funds chasing a small number of highly profitable MFIs. Commercial investors, social investors, international financial institutions, and government donors will all be placing their funds in the same institutions. The only way to break this logjam is for the MFIs that focus on serving the very poor to find ways to reliably demonstrate to the marketplace that they are reaching the clients they say they are and that, over time, those clients are moving from below to above the poverty line. This does not need to be done through large, expensive, and academically rigorous studies. Pick a few proxy indicators that reliably track poverty levels (housing, land ownership, education, nutrition, etc.). Ideally these measures would link in some way with the Millennium Development Goals (MDGs) to demonstrate the relevance of microfinance to the generally accepted goals of the development community. Measure all or a representative number of clients on these indicators when they come into the program and then periodically after that (when clients are reapplying for a loan or obtaining additional financial services). Then find a way to have this information independently verified so that it can be accepted by the marketplace. Fortunately, there is a lot of energy in the microfinance community on developing good social indicators that measure the poverty level of clients and indicate changes over time. USAID, together with the SEEP Network and the IRIS Center at the University of Maryland, has been developing poverty indicators and a social performance measurement tool that can be employed to provide an independent social audit of an organization. CGAP has developed a poverty assessment tool and an impact assessment resource center and is working on linking impact indicators with the MDGs. All of the microfinance rating agencies are developing tools for conducting social audits in addition to their financial and managerial audits. Many of these tools are based on the work developed by MFIs and MFI networks that have focused their efforts on serving the very poor and have measured their success by the impact they have had on their clients.[9] Perhaps the most promising tools are those developed by IRIS, GF, and ACCION that cost-effectively measure $1/day poverty. Some or all of these tools are likely to be certified by USAID by October 2006.

Two steps are necessary to complete this cycle and have this information become a standard part of investment decisions in the marketplace. First, more MFIs need to adopt, test, and refine these tools and publish their results in using them. MFIs that do this will develop a competitive advantage in the marketplace, for they will be able to provide the information that the social funds and government agencies need to demonstrate that the investments they make in these MFIs are having the desired social impact. Second, donors and social investors need to start requiring this sort of standardized information in their due diligence on MFIs before placing their investments. If just a few of the larger foundations and social investment funds started using a common format to evaluate the social performance of MFIs, they would make that tool the standard in the industry.

Once these steps are taken, the logjam should begin to break apart. MFIs will be able to distinguish themselves based on their target markets and range of impact. Subsidized money will flow to those institutions serving the hardest-to-reach segments of the population and those having the greatest social impact. Commercial money will flow to those organizations generating the highest risk-adjusted financial return. This will give incentives for MFIs focusing on the very poor to continue to innovate to reach further downmarket and expand their impact in order to achieve their mission and attract less costly funds with more flexible terms.

2. Support innovations that lower transaction costs. The key to reaching those at lower levels of poverty with commercial funding is to find ways to lower the costs of reaching those clients. New information and communication technologies show a lot of promise in this area but need further development and testing before they can be deployed on a wide-scale basis. Since some of the large private foundations that have recently begun to support microfinance made their fortunes in the technology field, this seems a natural area for them to support. Two specific areas of innovation appear to be critical to rapidly expanding the number of clients reached with microfinancial services. The first is the area of mobilizing savings. While those that provide safe and reliable savings services to the poor have demonstrated a very high demand for these services by the very poor, delivering these services through the traditional channel of branch offices with vaults and tellers is hugely expensive in relation to the average deposit balances of these clients. ATMs, smart cards, and wireless phones can be used to drastically reduce these costs, but they need to be tied to delivery mechanisms that are safe and reliable for the client and can operate in rural areas without consistent access to electricity. The second area is information management and processing. Over time one of the most valuable assets developed by MFIs will be the information they generate on their clients' borrowing and savings patterns. With credit and behavioral scoring systems, MFIs will be able to use this information to assess the appropriate services needed by a client. Right now much of this information gets lost because the institutions employing group lending methodologies tend to track borrowing and repayments at the group level rather than at the individual level. Each group keeps its own logbook of individual payments, but the institution, in an effort to simplify and save costs, enters only the group repayment history into its computer system. Tracking individual transactions would require that the system handle twenty to thirty times more entries compared with tracking group-level transactions. With the development of handheld devices, scanning technologies, and wireless communication, MFIs should be able to find a low-cost way of tracking this information on a regular basis. This will provide a much better understanding of what is happening in clients' lives and businesses, enabling MFIs to provide more targeted and cost-effective services.

3. Provide global foreign exchange cover. Many MFIs that could qualify for international social investment funds have difficulty finding ways to mitigate their foreign exchange risk. Some MFIs have utilized guarantee funds to avoid foreign exchange risk, but a single-country, single-transaction guarantee can be an expensive way of covering this risk. It is much less expensive when these risks are diversified across several countries. Bob Patillo suggests that one of the International Financial Institutions or one of the large private foundations should work with the industry and the foreign exchange markets to provide a diversified foreign exchange pool.

4. Help central banks rethink regulation. Regulation is another area where CGAP has provided an important service in developing consensus guidelines on good practices. However, most regulatory regimes are still stuck in brick-and-mortar thinking about geographic locations and fixed asset ratios. Regulators are struggling to catch up with new technology. Since microfinance has incentives to use new technology to lower costs, MFIs often find themselves hemmed in by regulations that no longer have any practical value. CGAP should sponsor regular interactions between regulators and the most innovative MFIs to see how regulation can play its critical role in protecting the financial system while also making room for those innovators who are finding ways to broaden that system.

CONCLUSION

The growth of microfinance over the last 30 years has come from those committed to reaching the very poor using marketplace tools to develop sustainable delivery systems. In this chapter I have let them speak for themselves because I wanted to celebrate the creativity and thoughtfulness that they have applied to this work. Now we have reached the point where MFIs are generating returns that the commercial sector has begun to notice. With access to commercial funds, these organizations can rapidly multiply the number of poor people they serve and provide their clients with a wider range of financial services. However, the job of innovation and risk taking is not over. Growth of the sector requires reaching out to poorer and more remote clients.

For MFIs focusing on reaching the very poor, the lesson of this research is clear: there is a large bank in your future. Either you must become one or you must partner with one. One way or another, you will need to gain access to the deposit base in your country. If others are already mobilizing those deposits, or have the tools to do so, then you need to find ways of working with them. You can match your expertise in providing low-cost ways of building and maintaining customer relationships with the very poor with their expertise in mobilizing and managing money. If others are not doing this, or if the financial system does not provide savings services for the very poor, then you may need to find low-cost ways to provide this service as well. This often entails becoming a regulated financial institution and incurring the greater costs of regulation. In the interim, international investment funds and guarantee funds can help provide capital that will support your growth.

The lesson of this research is also clear for commercial banks operating in developing countries: if you want to grow your markets, there is a focused microfinance operation in your future. Either you will need to find one to partner with or you will need to develop one. This will require both creativity and humility (characteristics not often associated with commercial banks). Banks need to understand that their traditional methods and practices do not provide a cost-effective way of reaching the very poor. In most cases they will need to work through other institutions that already serve this population and understand the tools, techniques, and attitudes needed to attract and maintain good customer relationships among the very poor.

And for the industry as a whole, this research points to several areas of innovation needed to bring commercial funding to the scale required for serving the hundreds of millions of very poor people who need access to financial services. Developing common tools for assessing the levels of poverty we are able to reach will help guide the use of scarce subsidies and fuel healthy competition between microfinance institutions. Support for the use of technology and alternative delivery mechanisms will help to drastically lower transaction costs, enabling us to reach poorer and poorer clients. With the right information and transparency in how it is reported, the use of commercial funds can initiate a virtuous cycle. MFIs successful in reaching the very poor can grow and generate profits that will attract more funding to reach more clients. Their success can attract new entrants to the field who can bring more funding with them. This competition can promote innovation, expand the range of services that MFIs provide, and drive down interest rates, leading to more people being served at lower cost. It also means that donor funds can be used where they are needed most, in hard-to-serve markets where profitable delivery models still need further development.

Notes

1. For more information on strategies for reaching this client group, see CGAP Focus Note No. 34, *Graduating the Poorest into Microfinance: Linking Safety Nets and Financial Services*, by Syed Hashemi and Richard Rosenberg (February 2006).
2. The people I interviewed and their institutions are listed below. These interviews all took place in March and April 2006. Biju C. Mathew of IMED in India conducted the interviews of Suvalaxmi Chakraborty and Sanjay Gandhi. All other interviews were conducted by the author. Unless otherwise noted, the information on the institutions given in the paper and the quotes from these individuals came from these interviews.

MFI/Bank Leaders
Godwin Ehigiamusoe, LAPO, Nigeria
Benjie Montemayor, OISASL, Ghana
John DeWit, Small Enterprise Foundation, South Africa
Francis Pelekamoyo, OIBM, Malawi
Carlos Labarthe, Compartamos, Mexico
Rose Castro, KMBI, Philippines
Angel De Leon, TSKI, Philippines
Suvalaxmi Chakraborty, ICICI Bank, India

Investors
Bob Pattillo, Gray Ghost Fund
Stephen Hardgrave, Omidyar Network

Raters
Damian von Stauffenberg, MicroRate
Aldo Moauro, Microfinanza
Sanjay Gandhi, MCRIL

Industry Supporters
Elizabeth Littlefield, CGAP
Syed Hashemi, CGAP
Bob Christen, Boulder Microfinance Institute

3. http://www.mixmarket.org/medialibrary/mixmarket/2004_MFI_Benchmarks[2].xls
4. Banco Do Nordeste, *Annual and Social Report 2004* and http://www. bnb.gov.br/ content/aplicacao/Produtos_e_Servicos/Crediamigo/gerados/O_que_e_objetivos.asp
5. Nair, Ajai. *Sustainability of Microfinance Self Help Groups in India: Would Federating Help?* Princeton, NJ: Princeton University, Woodrow Wilson School of Public and International Affairs, 2002, p. 5.
6. www.tufts.edu/microfinancefund/
7. CGAP Focus Note No. 36, *The Market for Foreign Investment in Microfinance: Opportunities and Challenges*, August 2005.
8. *MicroBanking Bulletin*, Vol. 11, 2005.
9. For more information on poverty assessment tools, see Zeller, Manfred, *Review of Poverty Assessment Tools*, Accelerated Microenterprise Advancement Project, United States Agency for International Development, 2004.

4

Building Domestic Financial Systems That Work for the Majority[1]

Women's World Banking

EXECUTIVE SUMMARY

Over the past ten years, microfinance has come of age. Poor women and men have shown that they are strong entrepreneurs, borrowers, and change agents. Outreach has expanded rapidly. Leading microfinance institutions, banks, and cooperatives have demonstrated how to provide efficient, responsive, and profitable microfinance services. Common performance indicators and standards have been established and are being used by networks, wholesalers, and raters. Microcredit has become microfinance, with a growing number of institutions responding to poor people's needs for a range of lending, savings, and insurance services. Key elements of the required policies, regulations, and institutional infrastructure have been agreed on and these elements have been adopted in several countries. New private actors have entered microfinance, with equity and loans made available by commercial and public sources.

Yet the microfinance industry is still in the early stages of development in most countries. While micro-lending outreach has expanded rapidly in the last ten years, from 9 to 90 million households, development has been uneven, and in most countries less than 10% of low-income entrepreneurs and households have access to basic lending and savings services. Our objective is for the number of households served to quadruple over the next ten years and, in all countries, for at least 50% of poor households to have access to financial services geared to helping them build income, assets, and livelihoods. In most countries this will require a three-pronged strategy.

High-potential specialized microfinance institutions will require financial and capacity building support that fits their stage of development. The entry of commercial banks into wholesale and retail microfinance must be promoted. And strong cooperatives and savings institutions must be encouraged to improve their organizations and product offerings.

In all cases, emphasis needs to be on developing the products that help low-income entrepreneurs and households build income and assets. Savings, business loans, insurance, and remittances for microfinance are all valued. MFIs will need to reinforce their knowledge of and connection with low-income clients to provide excellent service to this client segment. MFIs will need to become regulated or to build alliances to be able to offer savings products. Banks need to resist the temptation to fall into consumer and transaction finance. And most cooperatives and savings institutions will need to build more solid management and create stronger lending products. Technology applications, combined with solid risk assessment methods, will be key in reducing transaction costs and expanding outreach to underserved rural and urban clients.

Country microfinance strategies will constitute the core of a successful build-up of financial systems and services that work for the poor. Each country is different, but experience indicates the key elements that country stakeholders need to put in place, over time, to build a robust financial system that works for the majority. While some countries have implemented some of the essential measures, most countries have far to go. This chapter provides a general roadmap for country-level stakeholders—policymakers, microfinance institutions, banks, and supporters. Five levels of action will be key:

1. **Policies, regulations, and legal structures that work for microfinance.** The following dimensions need to be addressed in building policy regimes that work for microfinance: liberalized interest rates, responsive government and financial sector policies, performance indicators and standards, regulations and supervision capabilities for microfinance, a range of suitable legal structures, legal and judicial systems, government roles, and external support.

2. **Institutional infrastructure,** including technical service suppliers, wholesale finance, microfinance networks and industry associations, rating agencies and credit bureaus, IT platforms, payment systems, and business services, all playing effective roles in building standards, capacity, innovation, transparency, outreach, and performance in microfinance.

3. **Key financing instruments and arrangements,** including domestic savings mobilization, domestic wholesale financing, grants and soft loans for younger MFIs, bonds and securitization for the strongest MFIs, domestic equity financing, and guarantees—all supported by increased transparency and overall development of domestic capital markets. The chapter identifies

key elements of microfinance that regulators, wholesalers, and raters need to understand if they are to play effective roles in microfinance. Also provided is a tool to enable funders to assess the likely success of smaller microfinance institutions. Both tools are geared to help build domestic capital markets, moving from the dependence on hard-currency loans and equity funds that create serious risks for microfinance.

4. Retail capacity in microfinance. In most countries, microfinance institutions, banks, cooperatives, and savings institutions all have important roles to play. Each will require a thorough understanding of supply and demand, including supply by different sets of institutions of key products, for different income segments in rural and urban geographies. Each set of institutions will need to strengthen the commitment and competence of their boards and management to drive growth in microfinance. This chapter provides an analysis of competitive advantages, common pitfalls, and key measures of success in increasingly competitive markets for each of these sets of retail actors.

5. Products and processes that reflect the needs and wants of low-income clients and their households need to be developed. Regulated MFIs have been slow to build broad-based savings services, housing finance, and insurance. Commercial banks need to offer a range of products for lower-income entrepreneurs and households, with appraisal-based business loans forming the core.

Key areas for action to realize this massive expansion in outreach, product offerings, and impact over the next ten years include the following:

- Build retail capacity by microfinance institutions, banks, cooperatives, and new channels.

- Build the depth and diversity of products necessary to help low-income clients accrue income and assets.

- Build domestic and financial markets and industry infrastructure.

- Utilize best-practices methods and technology to cut costs and expand outreach.

- Develop permanent state policies and country strategies for microfinance.

- Mobilize new actors, and help them to play effective roles.

This chapter outlines the key building blocks in establishing country strategies for microfinance at six levels: policies, institutional infrastructure, domestic financing, retail capacity, product offerings, and impact on poor households (see Figure 4.1).

**Figure 4.1 Building Blocks of Domestic Financial Markets
That Work for the Poor Majority**

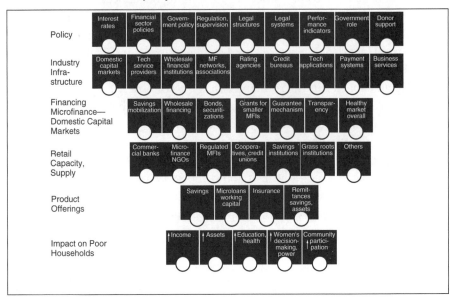

ACCOMPLISHMENTS AND CHALLENGES IN MICROFINANCE

The Most Important Accomplishments in Microfinance in the Past Ten Years

- *Poor women and men have shown the world that they are bankable, attractive customers of financial services.* Over the last decade, millions of poor women have led the way in showing that poor people are excellent clients and economic change agents—repaying their loans and using financial services to build income, assets, and a future for their families. Microfinance is seen as a central instrument in fighting poverty.

- *Leading MFIs and banks have developed profitable, sustainable microfinance services.* These institutions have demonstrated that providing financial services to poor entrepreneurs and households can be efficient, responsive, and profitable—with risk assessment methods used in individual and group lending to achieve high-quality portfolios without relying on conventional collateral.

- *Micro-loan outreach has increased dramatically.* Over the past ten years, the number of micro-loans has increased from about 9 million to over 90 million—far more than the 50 million projected in 1995 in the *Missing Links*[2] report.

- *An expanded range of institutions has evolved in many countries.* Strong regulated and unregulated MFIs, banks, and cooperatives have made major contributions to outreach, product development, and growth of the industry. A diverse set of global, regional, and country-level networks has emerged, playing distinct roles in capacity building, lateral learning, innovation, policy change, and mobilization of new actors. Global and local loan and equity funds are now financing strong MFIs on commercial terms.

- *We have moved from microcredit to microfinance.* Increasingly, retail institutions are responding to the demand by low-income entrepreneurs and households to provide the savings, insurance, housing finance, and flexible loans needed to build income and assets.

- *Microfinance is becoming integrated into financial systems.* Microfinance now is recognized as an integral part of a country's financial system—as well as a means to fight poverty. The core policies, regulations, legal structures, roles, and institutions needed to build financial services for the majority have been agreed to by key actors. Changes consistent with this good practice have been introduced in a number of countries.

- *There is agreement on key performance indicators and standards in microfinance.* The implementation of these standards by networks, rating agencies, and MFIs has resulted in improved performance and expanded financial markets for microfinance. Specialized rating agencies have helped build transparency and financing for microfinance. Mainstream rating agencies are beginning to take the microfinance industry seriously.

- *Awareness of microfinance has grown dramatically, with new private sector actors joining the industry.*

Challenges and Areas for Action in the Next Three Years

Retail Capacity

Retail capacity, the single biggest constraint to expanding outreach, needs to be increased. In almost all countries, less than 10% of low-income households have access to basic lending and savings services. In many countries, relatively few MFIs have built strong, sizable, sustainable operations; cooperatives are weak and banks are just beginning to consider microfinance as an attractive business opportunity. Actions to address this problem of limited retail capacity include reinforcing the capacity of high-potential microfinance institutions, mobilizing more mainstream banks for serious engagement in retail microfinance, strengthening cooperatives and other savings institutions, and encouraging the entry of new actors. Particular attention must be devoted to building retail capacity in countries and regions where market penetration is low, and to serving poorer clients. The deepening of outreach to more remote markets will require innovations in low-cost distribution channels to enable the delivery of cost-effective services. Organizational constraints to growth—governance, management, and change processes—will be particularly important to address if client-focused growth and change is to be achieved.

Microfinance Products and Processes

The focus needs to be on building financial services that help poor clients build income and assets. While the importance of savings and other asset-building products is recognized, many MFIs have been slow to expand voluntary savings services. Housing finance, health insurance, and mobilization of remittances for microfinance are still in the early stages. Retail institutions need to get better at customer research and product design to respond to different customer segments and the evolving needs of low-income women and their households. The focus needs to remain on income and asset-building products; consumer finance and transfer payments should not be treated as microfinance.

Transaction costs need to be reduced. Costs remain high despite productivity gains in the last decade. Operating costs need to be reduced through improved efficiency, scale, and application of technology to enable lower interest rates and to encourage entry by a wider range of retail actors.

Domestic Financial Markets

Domestic financial markets and local financing instruments need to be developed. With the focus on establishing global financing instruments in hard currency, most commercial financing has been concentrated in a handful of about 100 profitable MFIs. Many of the global, commercially oriented funds have been financed by bilateral and multilateral donors. It is now recognized that hard-currency loan funds create foreign exchange risks that threaten to undermine the viability of MFIs. Designed to compensate for underdeveloped local markets, these equity and loan funds can reduce the focus on building domestic financing instruments and arrangements. The global and regional equity funds can create artificial markets and put pressure on local MFIs to increase foreign control. The focus needs to be placed on domestic savings mobilization, local-currency loans to MFIs, bond issues and securitization for larger MFIs, and local equity markets. Commercial banks and cooperatives are more naturally integrated into domestic financial markets; banks can fund microfinance portfolios from general resources, and most cooperatives mobilize savings in excess of their loan portfolios. Promising small and medium-size institutions need a mix of seed capital, capitalization, local-currency loans, and capacity-building services to reach sustainable scale.

Country Strategies and Policies

Shared country-level visions and strategies are lacking in most countries. Policymakers, regulators, microfinance institutions, banks, and low-income people need to build a shared vision and strategy for microfinance. Policies, regulations, standards, financing, and capacity-building mechanisms need to be built. Each actor has a different role to play. These visions and strategies need to be home grown. They also need to reflect best practices and lessons learned over the past ten years with respect to the key elements needed in building financial systems that work for the poor majority.

Responsive policies and legal structures need to be established. Agreement exists among most key actors on the basic policies that must be in place to support the building of solid financial services for poor entrepreneurs and households. Yet few countries have put these core policies in place.[3] Institutions providing financial services to poor people need to charge relatively high interest rates to cover the high transaction costs of making small loans; competition and transparency, with liberalized interest rates, are key to success in building inclusive financial sectors. Micro-loans need to be treated as a distinct loan class, with strong risk assessment methodologies, excellent portfolio quality, and rigorous provisioning norms used to evaluate credit risk—based on the recognition that most poor clients cannot provide conventional collateral. Legal changes are necessary to enable a range of institutions to participate profitably in microfinance. Regulated and unregulated MFIs need to be integrated into financial sector policy.

Regulatory frameworks and supervisory capacity need improvement. With the increasing number of regulated institutions participating in microfinance, limitations in regulation and supervisory capacity now represent a key constraint. Regulators need to better understand risks in microfinance portfolios and institutions.[4] Some regulators hesitate to build legal structures and loan classes for microfinance because they lack the staff to supervise microfinance institutions and portfolios. With the arrival of Basel II, lenders are expected to demonstrate that clients have the capacity to pay, that overall portfolios are strong, and that borrowers provide collateral. It is important that policymakers and industry leaders build the case that good lending methodologies result in excellent portfolio quality in microfinance. Low-income clients have demonstrated their creditworthiness despite their inability to provide traditional guarantees.

Institutional infrastructure has to be built. In most countries improvements are needed in technical services, standards, ratings, credit bureaus, and financing arrangements for microfinance.

Performance indicators and standards need to be implemented. A much larger set of institutions engaged in microfinance must provide transparent reporting that is consistent with international definitions. Country, regional, and global microfinance networks and banking associations will continue to have important roles to play, along with specialized and mainstream rating agencies and market data services. Domestic wholesalers, rating agencies, and regulators need to deepen their understanding in order to make accurate risk assessments of microfinance institutions, portfolios, and transactions.

Solid, Dynamic Development and Support

Optimizing competitive dynamics. In an increasing number of countries, growing competition affords poor households greater choices. Competition creates pressure on retailers to improve efficiency, lower interest rates, and expand product offerings. This competition also creates risks of overindebtedness by poor clients, particularly if new entrants take shortcuts and do not assess the customer's capacity to repay. Many MFIs may find it difficult to compete with banks that have lower financing costs, a national branch infrastructure, and the ability to offer a range of products. Specialized MFIs will need to be expert in serving specific market niches, and they will need to forge alliances to offer a broader range of non-credit products. Competition among wholesale funders can reduce prices. However, competitive pressure among wholesalers could undermine quality if wholesalers are not strong in evaluating the risks of less established retailers. Increased competition creates pressure and potential for alliances, partnerships, and mergers. The entry of major commercial actors could result in new distribution systems and greater application of technology if these players invest in understanding microfinance and poor clients. Innovations are needed to lower costs and interest rates, as well as to dramatically expand outreach. It will be important to build a balanced microfinance industry with a range of institutional types serving different client segments.

Better industry intelligence. The industry needs a stronger understanding of local, regional, and global microfinance supply and demand, including by institution, by product offering, as well as by income, gender, and location of low-income households. The focus, however, needs to be less on static supply and demand data and more on understanding available retail capacity, customer patterns, and the dynamics of microfinance markets. Better information on customer satisfaction and impact is required.

Building needed public and private support. Government and private sector donors will continue to play important roles in supporting the build-up of retail capacity, product and process innovation, support services, and financial sector policies that meet the needs of microfinance. It is important that donors back a range of effective organizations and approaches, and that they see their roles as complementing private finance. Donor funding will remain important over the next decade in supporting capacity building and innovation in high-potential institutions of all sizes. Donors will need to encourage introduction of the needed policies and institutional infrastructure at the country level. Donors can help ensure that high quality standards are established and maintained, through direct funding and by backing strong wholesale and retail organizations. It is important that funders deepen their understanding of country realities to ensure that their support fits the stage of development of the microfinance industry.

BUILDING DOMESTIC FINANCIAL SYSTEMS FOR MICROFINANCE

Key Elements in Building Financial Sector Policies that Work for the Poor Majority

Nine measures are central to developing the policies, regulations, and legal structures needed for a robust financial system that serves the poor majority (see Figure 4.2). The following key points represent a consolidation of CGAP's eleven[5] and WWB's ten[6] key principles and policies for microfinance. They are geared to supporting the creation of a robust microfinance sector as an instrument for fighting poverty and as an integral part of financial systems. They are designed to help a range of institutions build responsive and sustainable financial services for large numbers of poor people.

Figure 4.2   Policy

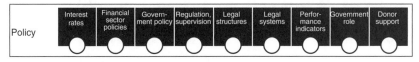

- *Liberalized interest rates for microfinance,* with no interest rate caps, relying on competition and transparency to lower costs and rates.

- *Inclusive financial sector policies* that incorporate measures to ensure responsive, solid services to the poor.

- *An explicit and supportive government policy and country strategy* for microfinance, incorporating objectives, key policies and support, and roles of key actors. The policy must make explicit what government and others will and will not do to support the build-up of a robust and sustainable microfinance sector. The vision and strategy should reflect consensus among key stakeholders.

- *Regulations and supervision capacities that respond* to the characteristics of microfinance. Micro-loans should be treated as a separate loan class. Risk assessments of micro-loan portfolios should be based on overall portfolio quality and loan methodologies, not conventional collateral. Strong capacities are necessary to enable effective supervision of microfinance portfolios and institutions.[7]

- *A range of suitable legal structures* must be in place to enable organizations of different types and sizes to provide diversified microfinance products in a sustainable way. Prudential regulation is needed for institutions that mobilize savings from the public. The available legal structures and regulations should enable small, medium, and large organizations to participate and compete effectively in microfinance, as regulated or nonregulated institutions.

- *Legal and judicial systems that support secured and unsecured lending.*

- *Common performance indicators,* definitions, and standards created for the range of institutions engaged in microfinance.[8]

- *The role of government as enabler,* promoting economic stability, liberalized interest rates, supportive policies, and private provision of retail microfinance.

- *Donor support to complement private capital* for financing younger institutions, capacity building, innovation, institutional infrastructure, and policy change.

Key Elements in Institutional Infrastructure for Microfinance

To establish domestic financial systems for microfinance, key policies and country-level strategies must be in place. Regulators, wholesalers, and rating agencies have to understand the key features of microfinance. Support institutions are needed to provide local financing, build capacity, reinforce performance standards and transparency, foster innovation, create scale economies, and construct the needed country-level policies and strategies.

Key institutions and services that will have to be in place to support the creation of solid, responsive retail capacity in microfinance include (see Figure 4.3)

- *Domestic capital market* development.

- *Technical service providers*—consulting firms, networks, associations, wholesale institutions, and other service suppliers to help microfinancing institutions generate operations, strategy, products, and financing.

- *Wholesale finance institutions*—public or private institutions that understand how to evaluate microfinancing institutions, require excellent performance, and provide financing and other services that fit the organization's stage of development and current needs.

- *Microfinance networks* and industry associations—to contribute performance standards, capacity, innovation, and policy change.[9]

- *Rating agencies*—both specialized and mainstream raters that understand microfinance.

- *Credit bureaus* that offer services adapted to the microfinance industry.

- *IT platforms* and the application of technology to microfinance.

- *Payment systems*.

- *Information and business* services for micro-entrepreneurs.

Figure 4.3   Industry Infrastructure

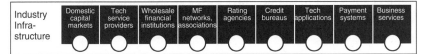

| Industry Infra-structure | Domestic capital markets | Tech service providers | Wholesale financial institutions | MF networks, associations | Rating agencies | Credit bureaus | Tech applications | Payment systems | Business services |

Figure 4.4   Financing Microfinance: Domestic Capital Markets

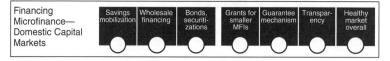

Key Domestic Financing Instruments and Arrangements

Key financial instruments and arrangements that are necessary if the domestic financial market is to respond to the funding needs of microfinancing institutions include (see Figure 4.4)

- *Domestic savings mobilization*—the most solid, stable means of integrating poor people and microfinance institutions into domestic financial markets

- *Domestic wholesale financing* with private or public banks making loans available for high-performing MFIs at different stages of development

- *Bonds and securitization* issues for the most advanced MFIs

- *Grants and soft loans* to enable high-potential MFIs to reach sustainable scale, and to support capacity building and innovation for MFIs at all stages

- *Guarantee mechanisms*

- *Enhanced transparency* with ratings, credit bureaus, and information disclosure

- *A healthy overall domestic capital market*, with active private equities and loan markets

What Regulators, Wholesalers, and Raters Need to Know about Microfinance

Regulators, wholesalers, and rating agencies need to understand key features of microfinance if they are to undertake effective risk assessments of microfinance institutions, portfolios, and transactions. Appendix C outlines these features:

- *Strong governance and management*, with the required mix of competencies.

- *Excellent portfolio quality and rigorous provisioning* in microfinance portfolios as a substitute for traditional collateral requirements.

- *Clear and sound credit risk policies and procedures*, with strong business and loan appraisal and risk management processes used by successful MFIs to achieve excellent portfolio quality in both good and bad times.

- *Limited documentation on underlying micro-loans.* Detailed documentation on individual micro-loans normally is not available, as lenders generally use smaller loans, simple cash flow assessment, and excellent overall portfolio quality to compensate for the lack of detailed accounting information and traditional collateral available from low-income entrepreneurs and households.

- *Strong, simple management information systems,* which serve as an early warning system and are a major contributor to effective risk management.

- *Financial profitability, with higher operating costs in microfinance.* Administrative costs are relatively high in microfinance, where the focus is on many small transactions. Microfinancing institutions are able to charge higher interest rates to cover costs and contribute to profits. Evaluators need to benchmark the performance of MFIs against similar institutions.

- *Asset-liability management*, and low foreign exchange risk exposure, are important to an MFI's success.

- *Strength in the ability to service clients*, not its balance sheet. Innovations in financing are often necessary to work around the limited capitalization of MFIs while leveraging their strengths.

- *Small, solid institutions.* Most MFIs are relatively small relative to conventional, regulated financial institutions. Risk and institutional size do not correlate in microfinance. Evaluators need to carefully weigh the strength of the board and of senior and middle management in achieving high performance. Evaluators also need to review the solid track record of strong MFIs and microfinance portfolios relative to those of large corporate entities. It is important that regulators benchmark and review the performance of an MFI against institutions of similar size.

MFIs should understand that regulators, wholesalers, and raters look for the following features in evaluating microfinance institutions and portfolios:

- *Strong governance and management*

- *Strong performance on portfolio quality*, plus profitability—with independent verification of results, through external audits and ratings

- *Strong information base*, with commitment to transparency

- *Ownership* structure, financial strength, and capital adequacy

- *Loan and client risk assessment methodology*

BUILDING RETAIL CAPACITY IN MICROFINANCE

Inadequate retail capacity is the most important constraint to the growth of microfinance in most countries. The main groups of retail institutions that have been engaged in microfinance are banks, regulated and unregulated microfinance institutions, cooperatives, and grassroots organizations. Savings banks provide limited savings services to large numbers of clients. Experience indicates that each set of institutions has an important role in building reliable services for low-income customers. Each group offers potential advantages to such customers and each is associated with different challenges.

Retail Capacity in Microfinance Institutions

In many countries, microfinance institutions have led the way in demonstrating how to build solid, responsive lending services for low-income entrepreneurs and households. At the same time, many MFIs have not demonstrated the capacity for growth and sustainability. Experience indicates that specialized institutions can have a significant impact if they are equipped with the following attributes:

- *A clear focus on and understanding of low-income clients*, with in-depth customer research and feedback

- *Dynamic, capable* top management, management teams, and governance

- *Focus on recruitment, training, and career development of line staff*

- *Proven core micro-loan products and methods*

- *Evolving focus on diversified product offerings* once excellence in micro-lending operations has been achieved

- *Emphasis on expansion of outreach and on achieving excellence* in efficiency, portfolio quality, and sustainability

- *Ability to mobilize loans, capital,* and grants to enable capacity building, innovation, and rapid expansion with progressive integration into domestic financial markets

- *Strong MIS, accounting, and internal controls,* fortified over time to accommodate growth and continuous improvements

Tools for Predicting the Success of Young MFIs[10]

It is important that smaller, younger MFIs get the support they need if they can demonstrate the potential to provide efficient, responsive services to substantial numbers of low-income entrepreneurs. Key characteristics that help determine the likelihood of success for smaller MFIs are provided in Appendix C. The core elements are

- Solid vision, strategy, and plan for growth

- Sound knowledge of and connection with low-income clients

- Firm governance, dynamic top management, and a capable management team

- Well-designed core products tailored to client needs

- Robust risk assessment methodology and good systems

- Focus on hiring and building line managers and loan officers

- Positive trends in outreach and performance

- Growth potential in competitive environments

- Legal structures that enable solid governance and expanded financing

MFIs in a Competitive Environment: Advantages and Pitfalls of Specialized Microfinance Institutions

With the entry of banks and the enhanced role of cooperatives in microfinance, regulated and unregulated microfinance institutions are each finding that they have some advantages. However, MFIs are also learning that they have several hurdles to overcome if they are to remain important sources of retail services for low-income entrepreneurs and households. These advantages and pitfalls are listed in Table 4.1.

Table 4.1   Advantages and Challenges for Microfinance Institutions

Advantages of Strong Specialized MFIs	Pitfalls That Could Undermine MFIs' Relevance
Mission-driven focus on serving low-income entrepreneurs and households	Lack of vision, management, and systems to achieve substantial scale[i]
Knowledge, connection, and commitment to low-income clients	Presuming to understand what clients want, becoming set in their ways and slow to change, growing insular in the face of competition
Experience with the products and risk assessment methods designed to respond to this client segment	Difficulty competing with the multiple product offerings of banks
Pro-poor branch structure in the barrios	Inadequate systems, use of technology, or finances to support rapid growth at lower costs
Skilled, dedicated, focused management and staff	Weaknesses in organization, governance, management, and staff undermining growth—or resulting in low quality if growth exceeds organizational capacity
Speed in providing core products	Legal and organizational difficulties in providing the range of products that low-income clients want
Lower direct operating costs on lending as a result of specialization, experience, and productivity	Higher financing costs, indirect costs, and overall cost structure relative to banks
Experience and comfort in dealing with clients that have no traditional collateral alternative guarantees	Difficulties with regulatory requirements
	Financial vulnerability due to donor dependence, legal structure, and failure to bridge gap with funders and raters on risk profile in microfinance

[i]Approximately 100 to 200 MFIs have achieved substantial scale and excellent performance, but there are tens of thousands of MFIs where internal management and governance issues have created serious constraints to growth.

Microfinance institutions will need to take several actions if they are to remain important players in the microfinance industry (see Table 4.2):

- *Strengthen customer focus,* customer research, and customer relationships. MFIs need to be the best at understanding the dynamics of low-income household economies and responding to what poor customers want.

- *Establish efficiency, commercial viability, and transparency.*

- *Achieve scale on core offerings* with emphasis on continuous improvement.

- *Reinforce and revitalize board, management, and staff* to strengthen their commitment to the mission and ensure the presence of skills, attitudes, and approaches to respond to clients and the changing environment.

- *Focus on the efficiency* of staff, branches, and the organization as a whole.

- *Verify that adequate systems* are in place, including MIS, controls, and risk management.

- *Seek to constantly learn, improve, innovate, and compete.*

- *Work to expand a stable, growing local funding base*—consisting of savings, borrowings, capital market instruments, and grant support for capacity building and innovation—to reduce average costs of funds and avoid foreign exchange risks.

- *Either become a regulated MFI and compete with banks on the high end of microfinance, or become very good at serving the low-income niche.*[11]

- *Be a key, cooperative player with other actors*—MFIs, banks, policy-makers, funders, poor women—in building the microfinance industry. Engender trust with all stakeholders.

Table 4.2   Key Challenges for Microfinance Institutions at Different Stages of Development

Key Measure(s)	Small MFIs (Less than 10,000 Clients)	Medium MFIs (10,000 to 50,000 Clients)	Large MFIs (Top 150, with over 50,000 Clients)
Clear client focus	Strong knowledge of, connection to, and mutual trust with low-income clients	Improve customer focus—with customer research, feedback	Redouble customer focus, to improve and expand product offerings
Leadership, management, organizational effectiveness	Strong, dynamic top management and solid governance—with strong core management team Strong vision, strategy, and plan for growth Focus on staff recruitment, training, and incentives, particularly of line managers and loan officers	Strong independent board of directors in place. Build strong senior and middle management, to enable growth to next stage. Intensive capacity building of staff	Strengthen board with strong finance capabilities Strengthen senior management, middle management, and board Institutionalize human resource development: staff recruitment, training, career development Consolidate organization, to facilitate rapid growth
Product offerings	Tailored loan products	Focus on rapid expansion in core lending products Begin to explore other product offerings Get connected on savings mobilization	Ensure that legal structure and organizational capabilities are adequate to offer multiple lending and savings products
MIS, systems, internal controls	Good basic systems	Improve MIS, ensure internal controls are in place	Strengthen MIS and controls—to accommodate growth and comply with regulations
Mobilizing and managing finance	Access a range of grant and low-cost loan funds, to build operations and portfolio to sustainable scale	Seek capital infusions Mobilize mainly commercial funding for portfolio expansion	Build capital base Integrate fully into domestic financial markets Ensure stable and growing source of local currency debt to full expansion
Branch network	Focus on head office and tight branch structure	Strategic branch expansion with rapid breakeven	Expand branch network, build lower-cost distribution systems
Risk assessment, operating efficiency and effectiveness	Robust risk assessment methodology Maintain excellent portfolio quality, positive trends in outreach, efficiency—demonstrating dynamism and solid management Ensure strong monitoring mechanisms	Get the basics right—take action to meet best-practices standards on efficiency, portfolio quality, and profitability Disciplined evaluation and supervision	Improve operating and financial efficiency—implementing best practices and integrating technology
Performance indicators and standards	Strong commitment to performance standards, transparency—for internal management and for funders	Transparency—publish performance using agreed-on indicators and definitions.; submit to networks and market databases Ratings by specialized agencies	Transparency—compliance with regulatory standards, regardless of whether MFI is regulated Rating by specialized and/or mainstream rating agencies
Use of leadership to build industry, policy change		Be a cooperative actor within the microfinance industry	Use leadership to work with policymakers, bankers, and other key actors to develop performance standards, innovation, and policy change
Legal structure	Legally established local institution	Explore becoming a regulated institution Build strategic partnerships	Ensure that regulated institutions, forge strategic alliances to enable savings mobilization and broad product offerings

Building Retail Capacity in Banks

Motivation of Banks Entering Microfinance

Many banks are recognizing the benefits of entering the microfinance market:

- Ability to access a major, profitable, untapped market—with many banks having excess liquidity and margins on traditional markets squeezed due to competition

- Ability to make use of best-practices methods in microfinance, often available from institutions in the same or a neighboring country

- Profitable opportunities in wholesale and retail microfinance

- Ability to tap the large and lucrative remittance flows going to low-income households

- Ability to demonstrate that the bank is contributing to the development of the country while making a profit

Advantages and Challenges for Commercial Banks

Mainstream financial institutions offer many potential benefits to low-income clients, shareholders, and the industry as they move to enter retail microfinance. At the same time, private and public sector banks face major challenges in providing microfinance services that are responsive to the poor. These challenges and benefits are summarized in Table 4.3.

Key Measures Required by Banks to Succeed in Microfinance

The most important measures that a commercial bank must take to succeed in retail microfinance are the following:

- Build and sustain top management's understanding of and commitment to microfinance.

- Design, pilot-test, and roll out microfinance products based on strong research on client needs.

- Build capacity in terms of management and specialized loan officers who understand this client group and know the methods for delivering micro-lending and other products.

- Focus on service, efficiency, and portfolio quality.

- Develop alternative, low-cost, reliable channels to sell a suite of financial products.

Table 4.3   Advantages and Challenges for Commercial Banks

Advantages of Banks	Challenges to Banks in Microfinance
Ability to offer comprehensive suite of products and services to low-income-clients, and adapting existing products to this new market, with regulatory facilities.	Most banks have not seen low-income entrepreneurs and households as attractive clients. Major changes in attitudes and organizational culture are needed. Deep customer research is required in order to design products and distribution systems for this new customer base. Banks that do not make the needed adjustments in culture, people, products, and systems will fail. Banks that offer consumer finance rather than appraisal-based products to low-income customers normally have serious repayment problems and fail to meet customer needs.
Ability to achieve large-scale outreach in a relatively short period using existing branch structures and financial strength to expand distribution channels.[i]	Many banks approach this segment tentatively, with cosmetic initiatives that do not put the weight of the bank behind serving this major new market.
Lower financing charges and the ability to allocate overheads result in the potential ability to charge lower interest rates to clients.	Need to make major front-loaded investments in people, methods, systems, and distribution channels, which can deter banks from entering.
Established systems, MIS, accounting, back office functions.	Time and focus are necessary to implement new staff structures, appraisal-based lending, productivity gains, and high portfolio quality, which can mean higher direct costs, at least in the early stages.
	Bank branch locations and staff are often not convenient or friendly to low-income borrowers.
More security on customer savings, with strong market presence, assurance of permanence, and deposit insurance.	
Ability to apply technology to products and distribution systems.	
Banks often have excess liquidity, with margins in traditional markets squeezed— allowing for new lending opportunities.	
Professional management with strong banking experience and the ability to roll out initiatives at scale.	Top and middle management may lack or be unable to sustain commitment to doing what it takes to successfully serve low-income clients. They may get in and get out. Commitment by top management is critical to the success of microfinance.
Interest in building wholesale finance, partnerships, strategic alliances with MFIs, strong potential for mutual learning.	The relative financial strength of banks may result in uneven and temporary partnerships with MFIs.
Competition among banks and with MFIs creates pressure for improved efficiency and reduced interest rates.	
Participation by banks adds to the clout and legitimacy of the microfinance industry.	Banks may be less willing than MFIs to use their influence on behalf of the country's microfinance industry.

[i]Many banks entering microfinance find that a period of two to three years is required for building operations, staff, methods, and distribution systems before significant scale is achieved, and some commercial banks have failed to reach scale because they have been unwilling to sustain these investments.

- Determine the best structure (e.g., a microfinance subsidiary or special-ized department) to combine specialized management and know-how with use of the bank's infrastructure.

- Learn from other banks and MFIs through exposure for senior man-agement, strategic partnerships, and specialized technical advice as needed.

Implications of Bank Entry into the Microfinance Industry

The entry by banks into retail microfinance creates major challenges for regu-lated and unregulated MFIs, and some risks for the microfinance industry as a whole. Banks that make needed investments in people, methodologies, sys-tems, and distribution will be able to serve higher-end microfinance clients. Banks can afford to pay line managers and loan officers more competitively. Banks have much greater financial clout to execute their expansion strategies. Banks that have financed MFIs may gather direct knowledge of microfinance clients and processes and then withdraw wholesale financing from MFIs. MFIs need to decide whether to compete head on, build partnerships, or establish niche strategies, focusing on lower-income or more remote clients. There is a risk that banks will seek out the good clients of MFIs and offer them more money without evaluating risk and thus create overindebtedness in clients. There is the risk that banks will employ consumer lending and use scoring methods without customer connection or evaluation, which could lead to low repayments. If microfinance by the banks is politically motivated and mandatory, there is a risk that banks will do microfinance poorly or not at all, with failed repayments and ruined markets. Poor women may be "scored out" of commercial bank financing. Banks may outperform MFIs in the short term and then decide to get out of the business, leaving low-income clients unserved. There is the risk that donors and governments will overesti-mate the participation of banks in microfinance, and not support the develop-ment of specialized MFIs.

Building Microfinance Capacity in Cooperatives[12]

Key success factors for cooperatives and credit unions in providing diversified financial products to low-income entrepreneurs and households include the following:

- Reinforce ownership and governance by members that yields solid accountability.

- Strengthen governance and management, with more reliance on professional management.

- Strengthen savings management and use.

- Design products to meet life cycle needs of members and potential members.

- Build a strong strategy for growth and sustainability.

- Tighten external supervision, with effective supervisory structures and capabilities in place.

- Build freedom from political interference.

- Commit to serving low-income clients—beyond the original member base.

- Develop and reinforce central mechanisms for liquidity transfers, and shared services and technology.

PRODUCTS AND SERVICES THAT POOR CLIENTS WANT IN MICROFINANCE

Key Features of Microfinance Products and Processes for Low Income Customers and for the Institutions Serving Them

While product features must be tailored to different markets and client segments, experience indicates that the following characteristics of microfinance products are important across markets:

Thorough customer research. Financial service providers must have thorough, ongoing customer research to design responsive products, to assess customer satisfaction, and to make needed adjustments to ensure competitive offerings.

Quick and convenient access. Low-income customers place strong value on ease and convenience of access, rapid approval, and limited paperwork in the area of financial products and services.

Simple product offerings, with some flexibility. Low-income customers value products that are easy to understand and use. Since they perform many small transactions, most microfinancing institutions have standardized offerings allowing them to provide products at reasonable costs. At the same time, clients value flexibility in loan size, in savings withdrawal, and in modular home improvement loans. Institutions that are able to provide adaptable products with flexible end use will have a competitive advantage.[13]

Multiple product offerings. Increasingly, low-income customers seek one-stop access to multiple products. The ability to save is as important as the ability to borrow. Flexible loan products, simple savings vehicles, housing finance, insurance, debit and credit cards, and remittance services are all viewed as important. Institutions that are able to develop the product offerings, databases, platforms, and distribution systems to offer multiple products will enjoy a great competitive advantage. MFIs that want to capture savings from the public and build the full range of product offerings will need to be regulated, or will need to establish collaborations with regulated institutions.[14]

Costs, interest rates, and fees. As a result of competition, low-income customers are becoming better educated regarding interest rates and fees in microfinance. Historically, the high rates on micro-loans have often been disguised through flat interest rates and non-transparent fees. While low-income clients are prepared to pay high rates to gain permanent access to loan products, they will shop around. The microfinance industry should provide clients with appropriate, simple, and clear interest rates and fee structures. Transparency in effective interest rates will require educating consumers and the media, and will yield pressure to increase efficiency and lower transaction costs.

Strong MIS and accounting systems. Such systems are critical in managing a large number of small transactions effectively. Some large microfinance institutions have been able to rely on decentralized, standardized manual systems. However, computerized MIS analysis is key to providing efficient services, creating client databases to facilitate tracking and flexible product offerings, and enabling rapid action in response to performance issues.

Poor-friendly staff and distribution systems. Many low-income clients do not trust or feel welcome by traditional financial institutions. Sound, specialized MFIs have an advantage in providing poor-friendly staff and branches in the barrios. Traditional financial institutions need new staff that understand these clients and products, and distribution systems that are dedicated to poor customers. Firm relationships of trust with clients have proven to be important to client development and retention.

Dynamic management, good governance, and permanent institutions. Customers accessing savings, insurance, and lending services will look for a solid, permanent, and responsive institution.

Financial strength and risk capital. These qualities are essential to support rapid expansion, product and process innovation, and loan products with longer terms to ensure growth and competitiveness.

KEY MICROFINANCE PRODUCTS AND SERVICES

Experience demonstrates that low-income entrepreneurs and households seek a range of financial products and services to build income and assets and to mitigate risks. The ability to save safely and access flexible micro-loans is a core need of low-income households. Life and health insurance and housing finance are important in helping poor households limit risk and build assets. Investment finance is important as micro-enterprises grow. Remittance flows and end use can be enhanced through measures that reduce fees on remittance transactions, and through the development of savings and investment products related to remittance receipts.

Micro-loans. In addition to the product features and capabilities listed above for all microfinance products, key needs for micro-loans include the following:

- *Rapid appraisal and approval of loans,* with efficient assessment of the implications of cash flow of the enterprise or household on individual loans, and on efficient group formation. Low-income customers increasingly expect their first loans within a couple of days, and subsequent loans immediately following the end of a preceding loan cycle. Lenders are finding that tailored loan scoring methods are helpful for repeat customers.

- *Minimal documentation and flexible guarantees.* Low-income customers are not able to provide detailed accounting, legal documentation, or traditional collateral. Lenders need to be able to assess risk without relying on these traditional means. Regulators must be able to accept excellent portfolio quality track records and appraisal methods as opposed to traditional collateral as appropriate means of risk mitigation in microfinance.

- *Service.* Microfinance institutions that want to compete with new entrants must be able to differentiate themselves with respect to customer service and connection.

- *Interest rates.* Transaction costs remain high in micro-lending. Microfinancing institutions need to deploy best practices in increasing operating efficiency, and seek means of applying technology to lower the costs of both transactions and distribution systems.

Figure 4.5   Building Core Microfinance Services: Focus on Income and Assets

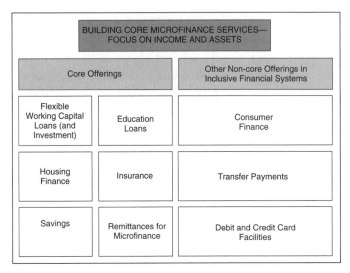

Microsavings. In addition to the features needed for all microfinance products, the following features are critical in providing responsive and efficient savings services to low-income households.

- *Security* for deposits associated with a solid, permanent, regulated institution

- *Convenient, safe branch locations* with hours of operation tailored to customers

- *Ease of withdrawal* on the basic savings product

- *Ease of opening a small savings account,* with low or no minimum balance, with incentives to clients to open accounts and to build balances that are economic for the institution

- *Simple short-, medium-, and long-term products,* with provision of education and incentives to move to longer terms, and marketing to encourage customers to save for different life needs

- *Competitive interest rates* paid to savers

- *Ability to attract both the poor and non-poor,* with products, incentives, and branches designed to attract larger savings accounts, to increase resources and reduce costs

Micro-insurance. Key features of insurance products include the following:

- *Excellent customer research,* since the uses and features of insurance products are extremely contextual

- *Focus on life and health insurance,* which are key products in most cases, with emergency, crop, and accident insurance important in some contexts

- *Simple, relatively standard products,* which are easier for customers to understand, can be understood and sold by non-specialized staff, and provide for cost-effective micro-insurance operations

- *Low premiums, clear terms and conditions, and quick claims procedures,* along with customer education on products, are features valued by low-income customers

- *The ability to assess, manage, and back actuarial risk,* which means that in most cases MFIs are the agents for a specialized insurance company

- *Ability to spread risks,* which requires a large, broad base of insured clients

- *Appropriate legislation* to enable strategic alliances between insurance companies and microfinancing institutions

Housing finance. Key features in housing finance for low-income households include the following:

- *Research* on how poor households invest in home improvement

- *Structured affordable offerings,* with products, monthly installment amounts, and rates based on an assessment of the capacity to pay of major customer segments

- *Focus on home improvement loans,* which clients indicate should allow them to complete construction in increments

- *Develop innovative ways to deal with security* and land title problems—using land titles where available, and considering transfer of land titles to women as a means of increasing security to the institution and the household

- *Make effective use of construction specialists* to increase value to the customer and to reduce risks to the institution

- *Ensure adequate financing and liquidity* to enable somewhat longer-term financing, with many home improvement loans made for three to five years

- *Price product to cover all costs*—with interest rates indexed

- *Lending to existing micro-loan clients* with solid repayment records or to new clients using microfinance appraisal methodologies

Remittances for microfinance. Banks and microfinance institutions that wish to capture international remittances as a source and service to low income customers need to

- *Charge lower fees* on remittance transfers, with transparency on fees and exchange rates.

- *Provide quick, reliable, and safe transfers* at both ends.

- *Make effective arrangements* with the bank or remittance companies in the sender country.

- *Offer savings accounts and other asset-building products* to remittance receivers, to encourage deposits and add value to customers. Housing finance with remittance transfers is a particularly promising product, as yet undeveloped in most markets.

- *Offer national distribution or obtain an agency agreement* with a remittance company that is able to handle accounts in different locations.

- *Secure access to international payments system,* to engage directly in remittance receipts, with better pricing to customers.

- *Employ solid information technology,* to lower costs and reduce cash-based transactions.

Key Nonfinancial Products and Services

Attention should be focused on nonfinancial services to increase the effectiveness of financial products and to increase prospects for low-income entrepreneurs and households to build income and assets. [15] Some of these services can be provided by financial institutions; others require linkages to specialized organizations. It is important to provide counseling and training for low-income women and men on financial planning, on the benefits of savings, and on how various financial products can be used to build income and assets. Commercial linkages, the introduction of higher value-added activities, and scale-up of production and marketing networks are needed to help low-income entrepreneurs, particularly women, enhance earnings opportunities. Health and education are key needs of low-income households that can be addressed through financial products and linkages to the provision of these services. Business advisory services and training become important for growth-oriented enterprises. Dealing with the legal barriers faced by low-income entrepreneurs, women, and households—property rights, land ownership, inheritance laws, and zoning—can increase the economic control and security of low-income people, particularly women.

THE ROLE OF GLOBAL PLAYERS

Multilaterals and Bilaterals

The most important contributions that multilaterals and bilaterals can make toward building microfinance services and systems in the next ten years are as follows:

- Provide and facilitate funding of promising organizations at different stages—directly and through second-tier mechanisms—with a strong focus on performance.

- Promote appropriate policies, regulations, and legal structures for microfinance.

- Act as catalysts in leveraging private capital and mobilizing new private actors.

- Finance technical services, training, and capacity building for institutions at different stages.

- Support the development of performance indicators and ratings in microfinancing institutions.

- Promote knowledge transfer and learning among MFIs, banks, regulators, and policymakers in order to disseminate innovations and good practice.

- Support foreign exchange risk mitigation instruments, to enable hard-currency funds to be converted to local-currency loans for MFIs at reasonable prices.

Multilateral and bilateral funders will need to make key changes to fulfill these roles. Those donors with specialized knowledge of financial sector policies for microfinance need to work closely with policymakers, practitioners, networks, and each other to build appropriate country-level policies, strategies, and support infrastructure for microfinance. International funders need to renew their commitment to providing appropriate financial support for the building of retail institutions at different stages of development, with grants and loan funds to build capacity and innovation. Funders need to be less restrictive concerning the end use of funds and more results-oriented, providing broad-based funding with clear, agreed-on performance measures. Donors either need to build solid internal competence in microfinance at the global and country levels or provide financing to networks and other structures to carry out capacity building, implement performance standards, and undertake policy change initiatives. Donors should support and disseminate innovation and best practices in the microfinance industry, back strategic alliances, and support the mobilization of new actors in microfinance.

Global Shapers of Financial Sector Policies

Global entities that shape financial sector policies include the International Monetary Fund, the World Bank, the Bank for International Settlements, regional banks, and some bilaterals. The following are key measures these entities should take to ensure that financial systems work for the poor majority:

- Support the development of inclusive financial sector strategies at the country level.

- Work with policymakers and practitioners to secure responsive policies, regulations, and legal structures for microfinance.

- Encourage public support of capacity building, innovation, and institutional infrastructure.

- Develop and track data on supply and demand of microfinance—by region, by income group, in urban and rural areas, and by institutional class—for various products.

- Work toward global agreement on the needed financial systems and standards that incorporate best practices and the nature of microfinance (e.g., Basel, international accounting standards).

- Provide and catalyze financing without distorting local markets.

Microfinance Networks

Global and regional microfinance networks need to take the following actions in supporting the development of the microfinance industry:

- Facilitate exchange of knowledge on product development and best practices.

- Distill and disseminate know-how, best practices, lessons, and cases.

- Provide technical services and training in high-value areas with impact for network members and for the industry.

- Help build and implement agreed-on performance indicators and standards.

- Work with network members and other key actors to influence global and local policies and systems.

- Help MFIs mobilize and manage commercial resources.

- Mobilize new actors for microfinance, and orient them to microfinance and constructive roles in building the industry.

Private Global Funders

Following are the areas in which private global and regional financial entities and funds can contribute in the next ten years:

- Build financial markets—with a focus on local-currency loans to MFIs, bond issues, and securitization transactions.

- Address the serious foreign exchange risk for international loans to MFIs. Hedging and guarantee instruments are necessary to encourage international funders to lend in local currency at reasonable prices. MFIs should avoid foreign exchange risk.

- Create private, local venture-type funds with social return expectations—equity, loans, domestic capital market instruments, and capacity building.

- Provide longer-term funding, with more attractive pricing, to promote rapid growth in MFIs through larger, more efficiently managed funds with better risk assessment.

- Build more commercial equity—domestic and international—with less reliance on donor funding.

- Promote better knowledge of capital markets, treasury management, financial risk management, and performance reporting among borrowing MFIs.

- Collaborate with established networks on due diligence and capacity building of MFIs.

A number of changes are needed if global and regional private funding sources are to fill their needed roles: the elimination of foreign exchange risks for MFIs, through funding in local currencies; simplified, responsive loan application procedures, due diligence contracts, and reporting formats; better terms and conditions on commercial loans; and support for treasury in establishment of guidelines on risk management for MFIs.

VISION FOR THE NEXT TEN YEARS AND KEY ACTIONS FOR THE NEXT THREE

Our Shared Vision for 2015

1. Poor people have built income and assets. Financial services are working effectively to support low-income entrepreneurs and households. Lending, savings, insurance products, and related services are being used to help poor people build incomes, assets, and livelihoods. The impact is being measured.

2. Client base has increased dramatically. The number of low-income households, individuals, and entrepreneurs making use of responsive financial products and services has quadrupled globally, and at least 50% of low-income households in all countries have access to financial services.

3. Microfinance institutions are solid, respected, influential players in domestic financial systems. Most of these players are fully integrated into domestic capital markets. Specialized MFIs have continued to innovate, demonstrating how to respond to the evolving needs of poor entrepreneurs and households.

4. A large number of regulated financial institutions have entered and expanded financial services to poor people—both directly and through partnerships with institutions specialized in serving the poor. Many banks have demonstrated how to provide a range of financial products and services to large numbers of low-income entrepreneurs, in a profitable and responsible manner.

5. Massive outreach at lower costs. Banks, MFIs, and new actors have used efficiency, innovation, and technology effectively to maximize outreach in rural and urban areas and to radically reduce transaction costs in microfinance.

6. **In almost all countries, effective policies and strategies** for financing the poor have been developed and implemented, with needed policies and support services in place and with appropriate roles played by government, regulated and unregulated financial institutions, funders, and low-income women and men.

7. **A coherent microfinance industry and movement exists.** Key actors are working together and fulfilling their roles in building financial services that help hundreds of millions of poor people build incomes, assets, and a better world.

Key Areas for Action

1. **Build retail capacity in microfinance.** High-potential large, medium, and small MFIs need backing in moving to the next stage. Commercial banks need to be mobilized and exposed to best practices in microfinance. Cooperatives and savings institutions should be encouraged to build efficient, dynamic services.

2. **Expand the depth and diversity of product offerings to low-income clients,** with particular emphasis on understanding and responding to what poor women want in microfinance. Core lending, savings, insurance, and remittance product offerings need to be developed. In constructing inclusive financial sectors, the focus on helping clients build income and assets should be maintained. The drift away from poor clients toward consumer finance, with less emphasis on financing economic activities and asset building, needs to be stemmed.

3. **Build domestic financial markets for microfinance.** Domestic savings is the key. Wholesale funding in local currency is needed. Bond issues, securitization, and equity will be required for specialized MFIs. Standards, ratings, and credit bureaus will facilitate capital access and expansion.

4. **Utilize technology to cut costs and expand outreach.** In microfinance, the key challenge is to reduce the high costs of many small transactions. Efficiency measures and the smart application of technology will both be important, if costs are to be reduced and if more remote networks are to be reached.

5. **Build permanent state policies and country strategies.** These country-level policies and strategies should reflect participation by all key stakeholders. They should incorporate objectives, key policies, support services, and roles. With agreement on the basic features of the policies, institutional infrastructure, financing, retail capacity, and responsive product offerings, it

should be possible for country teams to measure progress and to benchmark country policies and strategies. Appendix B lists some key elements in building an action-oriented country map of microfinance.

6. Mobilize new actors and help them learn the business and play effective roles in building the industry.

APPENDIX A: EXPERT GROUP MEETING + 10 PARTICIPANTS

MEMBERS OF THE EXPERT GROUP ON WOMEN AND FINANCE

Ms. Nancy M. Barry, President, Women's World Banking, USA

Ms. Ela R. Bhatt, FWWB and SEWA, India; WWB Board of Trustees

Dr. Mercedes P. Canalda, President, Banco ADOPEM, Dominican Republic; Chairperson, WWB Board of Trustees

Ms. Ruth Egger, Former Deputy Executive Director, Intercooperation, Switzerland

Ms. Elizabeth L. Littlefield, Director and CEO, Consultative Group to Assist the Poorest (CGAP), USA

Ms. Lisa Mensah, Executive Director, Initiative on Financial Security, Aspen Institute, USA

Dr. Karl Osner, Founder and former Managing Director, Deutsche Kommission Justitia et Pax, Germany

Mr. Richard Patten, former Project Associate, HIID/BRI Banking Project, Bank Rakyat Indonesia (BRI), Indonesia

Ms. Elisabeth Rhyne, Senior Vice President, International Operations, Africa, and Senior Vice President, Research, Development & Policy, ACCION International, USA

Ms. Deanna S. Rosenswig, Chair, WWB Advisory Board, Canada

Ms. Leila Webster, Senior Program Officer, IFC/World Bank, USA

Mr. Lawrence Yanovitch, Director of Policy and Technical Assistance, FINCA International, Inc., USA

Mr. Pedro Aspe,* Chairman and CEO, Protego, Mexico; and Former Finance Minister of Mexico

Professor Malcolm Harper,* Professor Emeritus, Cranfield University, UK

Mr. Teckie Ghebre-Medhin,* Senior Advisor Economic Empowerment, United Nations Development Fund for Women (UNIFEM), USA

  *Long-distance participant

UN INTERNATIONAL YEAR OF MICROCREDIT ADVISORS

Mr. Fouad Abdelmoumni, Director, Al Amana, Morocco; WWB Board of Trustees

Mr. Gregory Casagrande, Founder, Chairman, and President, South Pacific Business Development Foundation, Samoa

Mr. In Channy, General Manager, ACLEDA Bank Limited, Cambodia

Dr. Leonor Melo de Velasco, President, Fundación Mundo Mujer-Popayán, Colombia

Ms. Diana Medman, Chairperson, Russian Women's Microfinance Network, Russia; WWB Board of Trustees

Ms. Marilou H.G.E. van Golstein Brouwers, Managing Director of International Funds, Triodos Bank NV, The Netherlands; WWB Board of Trustees

Mr. René Azokli,* Director, PADME, Benin; WWB Board of Trustees

HRH Princess Máxima,* Advisor for the International Year of Microcredit 2005, The Netherlands

Mr. Diederik Laman Trip,* Advisor for the International Year of Microcredit on behalf of ING, The Netherlands

   * Long-distance participant

OTHER LEADERS

Dr. Clara Serra de Akerman, President, Fundación WWB Colombia; Board of Trustees

Mr. Fernando Esmeral Cortes, Vice President, BANCOLDEX, Colombia

Ms. K. Burke Dillon, former Executive Vice President, Inter-American Development Bank (IDB), USA; WWB Board of Trustees

Mr. Ranjit Fernando, former Managing Director, National Development Bank (NDB) of Sri Lanka; WWB Board of Trustees

Ms. Maricielo Glen de Tobon, President, Corporación Mundial de la Mujer Colombia, Colombia; Executive Director, Federación Latinoamericana de Bancos (FELABAN); WWB Board of Trustees

Mr. Madhav Kalyan, Country Manager and Chief Representative, ICICI Bank Limited, USA

Mr. Asad Mahmood, Director, Community Development Group, Deutsche Bank, USA

Mr. Agus Rachmadi, Senior Microfinance Specialist, Bank Rakyat Indonesia (BRI), Indonesia

Mr. Alvaro Ramirez, Chief, Micro, Small and Medium Enterprise Division, Inter-American Development Bank (IDB), USA

Ms. María Victoria Sáenz, Operations Specialist, Multilateral Investment Fund, Inter-American Development Bank (IDB), USA

Mr. Abdoul Anziz Said Attoumane, Executive Director, Africa Microfinance Network (AFMIN), Cote d'Ivoire

Ms. Marilou Uy, Sector Director, Financial Sector Operations and Policy, World Bank, USA

Ms. Jayshree Vyas, Managing Director, SEWA Bank, India; WWB Board of Trustees

Mr. Krisna Wijaya, Managing Director, Bank Rakyat Indonesia (BRI), Indonesia

Ms. Suzanne Nora Johnson,* Vice Chairman, Goldman Sachs Group, Inc; Friends of Women's World Banking Board of Trustees

Nations Development Fund for Women (UNIFEM), USA

*Long-distance participant

UN OFFICIALS

Mr. José Antonio Ocampo, Under-Secretary-General for Economic and Social Affairs, United Nations; former Finance Minister, Colombia

Mr. Barry Herman, Senior Advisor, Financing for Development Office, Department of Economic and Social Affairs (DESA)

Ms. Kathryn Imboden, Senior Policy Advisor, United Nations Capital Development Fund (UNCDF)

Mr. Peter Kooi, Director, Special Unit for Microfinance, United Nations Capital Development Fund (UNCDF)

Mr. Donald Lee, Chief, Poverty Eradication and Employment Section & Focal Point, Department of Economic and Social Affairs (DESA)

WWB TEAM MEMBERS WHO CONTRIBUTED

Mr. Frank Abate, Policy Coordinator

Ms. Nicola Armacost, Manager, Linkages and Learning

Ms. Mariama Ashcroft, Relationship Manager—Africa

Ms. Mercedes Benavides, Relationship Manger—GNBI

Ms. Rocio Cavazos, Financial Products and Services Analyst

Mr. Donald Creedon, Desktop Publishing Specialist

Ms. Dédé Ekoué, Relationship Manager—Africa

Ms. Wanjiku Kibui, Director Relationship Management

Ms. Sasha Laumeister, Desktop Publishing Specialist

Ms. Sarah Leshner, Executive Assistant to the President

Ms. Cathryn Mattson, Chief Operations Officer

Ms. Ann Miles, Manager, Financial Products and Services

Ms. Nandini Pandhi, Linkages and Learning Associate

Appendix B: Vectors of Action in Microfinance—Constructing a Country Map

In assessing the status of key areas for action in identifying country strategies for microfinance, stakeholders need to review performance in the areas illustrated in Figure 4.6 and listed in Table 4.4.

Table 4.4 Vectors of Action in Microfinance

Key Vector	Parameter
Outreach	Country, region Rural, urban Income level Products supplied Supply vs. demand
Client-responsive services: product range	Core working capital lending product Savings—short-, medium-, long-term Insurance—life, health

Retail capacity, diversity of legal structures in microfinance	Number of, outreach by MFIs, cooperatives, banks, overall and by geography, with
	     Over 500,000 borrowers, clients
	     100,000 to 500,000
	     50,000 to 100,000
	     20,000 to 50,000
	     10,000 to 20,000
	     Under 10,000

Policies, regulations, legal structures	Compliance relative to nine key points
Institutional infrastructure	Relative to list provided on pages 000–000
Product diversification	Average number of products per client by institution
Financing microfinance—integrated into domestic financial markets	Percentage of finance from savings and commercial sources, by size of MF
Performance standards, transparency	Number of MFIs publishing performance, rated, in network that verifies and publishes performance Consistent set of MF indicators used for regulated and unregulated MFIs Benchmarking

Figure 4.6   Building Blocks of Domestic Financial Markets That Work for the Poor Majority

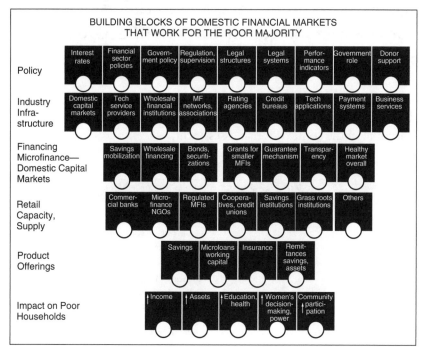

APPENDIX C: Characteristics of MFIs That Regulators, Wholesalers, and Rating Agencies Must Understand to Perform an Effective Risk Assessment

Table 4.5 details the characteristics distinguishing MFIs from banks and other traditional financial institutions. It is essential that these differences be taken into account in the context of risk assessment.

Table 4.5   MFI Risk Assessment: Key Characteristics to Consider

Characteristic	Key Indicator	How It Differs from Traditional Financial Institutions
Governance and management structures and competencies		MFIs need a strong board and management team, with members who have competencies in microfinance, banking, and finance and a connection with low-income clients.
Portfolio quality		Normally, MFI portfolio quality should exceed the quality of commercial banks' overall loan portfolios. Since low-income clients lack traditional collateral, evaluators need to put more weight on portfolio quality and provisioning in evaluating an MFI. Look for • <3%: normal • 3–5%: below normal • 5%: worrisome
	Write-off ratio	Look at write-offs in tandem with PAR to ensure that an MFI is not hiding portfolio problems with aggressive write-offs.
	Risk coverage ratio	Since there is no real collateral on micro-loans, provisioning should normally be very conservative, at levels of 100% of the full balance of delinquent loans over 30 days.
Cost structure and productivity	Operating expense ratio	MFIs normally have a substantially higher operating expense ratio than do conventional financial institutions—generally no higher than 20% of average gross portfolio (as opposed to the 2% to 4% found in traditional financial institutions) for institutions that have achieved some scale (e.g., over 10,000 micro-borrowers and outstanding portfolios of over US$4 million). This is partly due to the very small average loan size—normally between US$200 and US$1,000.
	Loan officer productivity	The rate has reached 350 to 500 borrowers per loan officer in most markets. It is also important to look at the overall productivity of personnel, including indirect.

Table 4.5   MFI Risk Assessment: Key Characteristics to Consider *(Continued)*

Characteristic	Key Indicator	How It Differs from Traditional Financial Institutions
	Funding expense ratio	A key risk variable relates to the ability of the MFI to charge what it costs to make a loan—operating costs, including provisioning, plus financing costs—and make a reasonable profit. MFIs tend to have higher financing costs, more expensive commercial capital access, and low or no reliance on mobilizing savings.
Profitability	Portfolio yield	Normally higher than 40% per year, but varies widely by region; must be understood relative to prevailing interest rates. Portfolio yield is an initial indicator of an institution's ability to generate revenues with which to cover operating and financial expenses. Tends to be higher among MFIs.
	Margins	Between costs and interest rate yields, a measure of the profitability of the portfolio; should normally be about 10%. Patterns over time are important: an abrupt reduction in margins could indicate problems. For NGOs for which retained earnings are the main means for equity growth, healthy margins are particularly relevant.
	Return on assets	
	Return on equity	
Regulatory environment	Interest rate ceilings	MFIs must be able to charge relatively high interest rates to cover the high costs associated with many small transactions. Interest rate ceilings can undermine viability.
	Asset classification and loan loss provisioning	In many countries, financial sector policies, regulations, and legal structures have been created for conventional banks and do not yet reflect the needs and realities of MFIs (e.g., asset quality ratings should not be too heavily weighted on collateral, but rather should look at repayment capacity/history; MFIs prefer more conservative reserve rates for their business).
	Reporting requirements	Regulations can have a dramatic impact on the cost structure and risk profile of the microfinance industry (e.g., the remote locations where MFIs operate make it very difficult to comply with some reporting requirements).
	Tax treatment	MFIs may have substantial tax advantages over conventional commercial institutions.

Table 4.5   MFI Risk Assessment: Key Characteristics to Consider *(Continued)*

Characteristic	Key Indicator	How It Differs from Traditional Financial Institutions
Legal structure	Most MFIs are not-for-profit organizations, without owners	While MFIs may legally be nonprofits, many are profitable and successful institutions, with long track records. Many have strong governance, with highly professional boards with financial expertise. The lack of owners does not preclude strong governance, oversight, and processes. Successful MFIs generally use the top auditing firms operating in their country.
Credit methodology	Solid, documented, and deployed methodology including the following features: • For individual loans, simple appraisal of the cash flow of the enterprise and household (often in combination with a guarantor) • For group lending, strong peer pressure and/or group guarantees In both cases, • Small, short-term initial loans • Personal contact by loan officers with customers, at least on the first few loans • Systems enabling decentralized loan processing and approval, under solid guidelines • Quality MIS to track loan approvals, disbursements, repayments	Unlike consumer lending, in individual micro-lending methodologies, MFIs measure the cash flow of the business and the household, as a key means to evaluate loan repayment capacity and reduce risk (often loans are structured so that approximately 50% to 75% of free cash flow is considered for loan repayment). MF clients generally do not have formal financial statements, so a sound analysis is key. In group lending methodologies strong peer pressure and/or group guarantees is the key for loan repayment. In both cases, early loans are normally short term and of small size, in order to reduce risk and develop a credit history for future reference. Since MFIs manage a large number of small transactions, it is usually impractical to require that underlying loan documentation with client financials be provided to regulators or wholesalers. Although sound documentation is key to the appraisal of larger loans, the person analyzing an MFI needs to be certain that the MFI uses a sound lending methodology, regardless of documentation, to evaluate clients' ability and willingness to repay. Regulators, wholesalers, or raters need to understand what constitutes good micro-lending methods and systems.
Balance sheet structure	• Portfolio/assets ratio tends to be higher • Higher capitalization and lower leverage • Lack of savings mobilization	MFI operations focus primarily on MF loans. Since these loans are predominantly short-term, this helps the MFI's liquidity profile. Given the historical difficulty in accessing loans and the fact that their initial funding often came from donors, MFIs tend to be highly underleveraged. Their high profitability and reinvestment of earnings to fund their portfolio growth contribute to their high capitalization. MFIs that are unregulated should not mobilize voluntary savings.

Table 4.5   MFI Risk Assessment: Key Characteristics to Consider *(Continued)*

Characteristic	Key Indicator	How It Differs from Traditional Financial Institutions
Small size of most MFIs	Since most MFIs are still small, with portfolios of under US$100 million, the availability of ready information on key financial and performance aspects may be less readily available than for large, conventional financial institutions. Some of the largest, most successful MFIs in Asia rely mainly on manual MIS—and achieve excellent efficiency, portfolio quality, and profitability.	Most MFIs are substantially smaller than conventional financial institutions. Evaluators need to recognize that smaller MFIs can be solid, and that a large MFI in today's market would be one with 100,000 clients and a lending portfolio of US$30 to US$100 million. While use of IT is becoming more prevalent and adaptable in microfinance, evaluators need to avoid judging the quality of the institution by the ready availability of data on all aspects normally available in banks.
Systemic risk	Ability to weather economic downturns and volatility	Most successful MFIs show less volatility in profitability and other performance indicators than do banks in times of economic recession, banking system crisis, and other adversities.
Risk management	• Credit risk • Market risk • Foreign exchange • Interest rate • Operational risks • Liquidity risk	Credit risk is generally lower for MFIs, especially given their high loan diversification and strong credit methodology. MFIs diversify the risk of their portfolio by having large numbers of small borrowers, operating in a diversity of sectors and geographies. Banks and other large businesses are in a much better position to hedge and otherwise cover any FX risk. Normally, a sizable MFI should not take FX risk on more than 10% of its equity. The short-term nature of MF loans and their healthy profit margin often mitigate against any mismatch in interest rates. MFIs often lack the access to backup lines of credit that more traditional banks have for liquidity. Given the short-term nature of MF loans, MFIs generally are well positioned relative to liquidity.
Portfolio diversification	• Client • Sector • Regional	MFIs spread risks over very small transactions.

Table 4.6 outlines and summarizes the criteria that can be used in evaluating and predicting the success of relatively small MFIs.

Table 4.6   Tool for Evaluating and Predicting the Success of Relatively Small MFIs (Less than 10,000 Microfinance Clients)

Internal Factors—Qualitative	
Institution age	• Number of years in operation—tracked with growth in outreach and performance improvements
Leadership, management, and vision	• Strong, dynamic, qualified top management, with track record of building high-growth organizations • Qualified, committed management team and line staff; strong incentives • Strong staff commitment to institutional mission, vision, and objectives • Strong vision, mission, strategy and business plan
Strong governance and organization	• Strong and active board of directors, with skills and experience in microfinance, banking, finance, and accounting • Clear and independent governance structure • Strong commitment by the board to the organization's mission and vision • Strong fiduciary responsibility • Legal structure which enables strong governance and expanded financing
Client-responsive products and processes	• Strong demonstrated knowledge of and connection with low-income clients • Well-designed core products tailored to client needs • Robust risk assessment methodology and systems • Strong representation of board and management in the market • Involvement of board, management, and staff in local leadership
Internal Factors—Quantitative	
Excellent portfolio quality	• PAR @ 30 days under 5% • Write-off ratio • Risk coverage ratio
Rapid growth	• Positive, relatively rapid growth rate in number of clients and portfolio volume higher than the growth rate for institutions of a similar size in that market.
Improving efficiency	• Operating cost/average gross portfolio • Cost per borrower • Number of borrowers per staff • Ratio of direct vs. indirect expenses Look for strong absolute and relative performance, compared to institutions of similar size and type, and improvement over last three years
Client retention and acquisition	• Client retention ratio, trends • New client acquisition ratio, trends
Profitability trends	• Portfolio yield, margins—performance, trends • ROA, ROE—performance, trends
External Factors	
Market potential	• Size of the untapped market
Market position and trend	• Number of competitors • Market share and ranking per competitor • Growth rate of each competitor
Availability and access to capital	• Strength of local banking system (for on-lending to MFIs) • Access to donor capital • Access to international capital

Notes

1. This chapter, prepared by Women's World Banking, is a slightly modified version of the Expert Group + 10 report "Building Financial Systems That Work for the Majority" (see the website http://www.swwb.org/English/PDF/Expert_Group_Booklet.pdf). In April 2005 WWB convened forty of the world's microfinance leaders to deliberate on the achievements of the past decade, the challenges for the future, the actions needed to meet those challenges, roles for key actors, and a shared vision for the next ten years (see Appendix A for a complete list of these leaders). The group produced a consensus document, which is the basis for this chapter.

2. See the website http://www.swwb.org/English/PDF/Expert_Group_Booklet.pdf.

3. While these core features of financial systems that work for the majority are generally agreed on, their application and the sequencing of their implementation will vary in response to country conditions and the stage of development of the microfinance industry.

4. More work is needed on key policy and regulatory aspects that relate to savings, insurance, and other new products beyond loans.

5. See the CGAP website *Key Principles of Microfinance*, http://www.cgap.org/portal/binary/com.epicentric.contentmanagement.servlet.ContentDeliveryServlet/Documents/KeyPrincMicrofinance_CG_eng.pdf.

6. See the WWB website *Building the Paradigm and Policy Framework for Microfinance*, http://www.swwb.org/English/2000/building_policy_framework_for_microfinance.htm.

7. In many countries government policymakers and central bankers have determined that the majority of MFIs should remain unregulated. This in part reflects real constraints in central banks to regulate and supervise large numbers of small institutions as well as the desire to avoid cost burdens on small MFIs.

8. In some countries performance standards have been developed to increase transparency and motivate a range of retail providers to improve performance. This system of "self-regulation" is probably most appropriate for the large number of small microfinancing institutions. However, when voluntary savings are being mobilized, more formal regulation is recommended.

9. Microfinance networks and banks have important roles to play in building transparency and pro-client codes of conduct for the microfinance industry.

10. Among MFIs that have not achieved scale, it is important to evaluate promise so that scarce resources are used effectively and to ensure that the next generation of MFIs receive the support they need.

11. Some leading microfinance NGOs have decided to become regulated for-profit financial institutions; the advantage of this structure is that the MFI can provide a relatively full range of lending and savings services and can more easily mobilize resources from domestic and international sources. On the other hand, regulated for-profit institutions can face higher costs, and some private shareholders may push the institutions to focus less on low-income clients.

12. Credit and savings cooperatives often have strong advantages in mobilizing savings, particularly from rural households. In some countries cooperatives have faced severe problems involving governance, management, and portfolio quality. Where these problems have been addressed, cooperatives have been key actors in providing broad-based lending and savings services to low-income households. Post office savings banks and other savings institutions have proven to be effective in mobilizing savings, but most have not been able to develop lending and other key product offerings for low-income entrepreneurs and their households.

13. Various forms of group lending products have proven important in providing very poor borrowers with initial access to small loans. In some areas group lending has also been an important means of building confidence and capabilities among low-income women. Over time, as the economic situation of low-income people improves, many of them come to prefer individual loans. Individual lending methodologies enable lenders to evaluate the cash flow of enterprises and households, which is an important means of mitigating and managing risk.

14. MFIs find that they need to make major changes in staff capabilities, customer interface, and distribution systems in order to provide the multiple product offerings that low-income clients increasingly demand.

15. Some of the very poorest households will not be viable clients of microfinance services since their economic activities do not enable them to repay interest-bearing loans. Other services are required for this group to enhance their economic opportunities and provide a social security net.

Selected Bibliography

Dewez, David, Karen Horn-Welch, and Patricia Lee Devaney. (2003). *ACCION Poverty Outreach Findings and Analysis: SOGESOL, Haiti.* Boston: ACCION. (A condensed version of the report is available as *ACCION InSight* No.8, www.accion.org/insight.)

Gibbons, David, and Anton Simanowitz, with Ben Nkuna. (1999). *Cost Effective Targeting: Two Tools to Identify the Poor.* CASHPOR-SEF Operational Manual. CASHPOR Technical Services.

Graham, Carol. (Forthcoming). "The Economics of Happiness." In Steven Durlauf and Larry Blume, eds., *The New Palgrave Dictionary of Economics,* 2nd ed.

Hatch, John. (2002). *Towards a Cost-Effective System for Measuring the Social Performance of FINCA Programs.* FINCA Concept Paper.

Henry, Carla, Manohar Sharma, Cecile Lapénu, and Manfred Zeller. (2003). *Microfinance Poverty Assessment Tool.* Consultative Group to Assist the Poorest (CGAP), http://www.cgap.org. Washington, DC: World Bank.

Horn-Welch, Karen. (2002). *ACCION Poverty Assessment Framework. ACCION InSight* No.1, www.accion.org/insight. Boston: ACCION.

Horn-Welch, Karen, and Patricia Lee Devaney. (2003). *ACCION Poverty Outreach Findings and Analysis: Mibanco, Peru.* Boston: ACCION. (A condensed version of this report is published as *ACCION InSight* No. 5, www.accion.org/insight.

Karshenas, Massoud. (2004). *Global Poverty Estimates and the Millennium Development Goals: Towards a Unified Framework.* Geneva: International Labor Organization (ILO), Employment Strategy Department.

Khandker, Shahidur. (2005). *Microfinance and Poverty: Evidence Using Panel Data from Bangladesh.* World Bank Economic Review.

McNelly, Barbara, and Christopher Dunford. (2002). "Concept Paper: Testing Low-Cost and Management-Oriented Poverty Verification Measures." Paper prepared by Freedom from Hunger for presentation at SEEP Annual General Meeting, October 2002.

Reddy, Sanjay G., and Thomas W. Pogge. (2003). "How *Not* to Count the Poor." Unpublished mimeograph, Columbia University, http://www.socialanalysis.org.

Sen, Amartya. (1982). *Poverty and Famines: An Essay on Entitlements and Deprivation.* Oxford: Clarendon Press.

Schreiner, Mark. (2006). "A Poverty Scorecard for India." Unpublished manuscript. (See also reports by the same author on the Philippines, Mexico, and other countries at http://www.microfinance.com).

Zeller, Manfred. (2004). *Review of Poverty Assessment Tools.* Report submitted to IRIS and USAID as part of the Developing Poverty Assessment Tools Project, http://www.povertytools.org.

Zeller, Manfred, Gabriela V. Alcaraz, and J. Johannsen. (2005a). *Developing and Testing Poverty Assessment Tools: Results from Accuracy Tests in Bangladesh*. Final report. College Park: University of Maryland, IRIS Center, http://www.povertytools.org.

Zeller, Manfred, Julia Johannsen, and Gabriela V. Alcaraz. (2005b). *Developing and Testing Poverty Assessment Tools: Results from Accuracy Tests in Peru*. Final report. College Park: University of Maryland, IRIS Center, http://www.povertytools.org.

Zeller, Manfred, and Gabriela V. Alcaraz. (2005c). *Developing and Testing Poverty Assessment Tools: Results from Accuracy Tests in Uganda*. Final report. College Park: University of Maryland, IRIS Center, http://www.povertytools.org.

Zeller, Manfred, and Gabriela V. Alcaraz. (2005d). *Developing and Testing Poverty Assessment Tools: Results from Accuracy Tests in Kazakhstan*. Final report. College Park: University of Maryland, IRIS Center, http://www.povertytools.org.

Index

About the Authors

Sam Daley-Harris

Sam Daley-Harris is Director of the Microcredit Summit Campaign and and founder of RESULTS Educational Fund, which organized the February 1997 Microcredit Summit held in Washington, DC. The Summit seeks to reach 175 million of the world's poorest families, especially the women of those families, with credit for self-employment and other financial and business services by 2015 and ensure that 100 million of these families rise above the US$1/day threshold.

Mr. Daley-Harris is also founder and President of RESULTS, an international citizens' lobby dedicated to creating the political will to end hunger and the worst aspects of poverty. Mr. Daley-Harris is author of *Reclaiming Our Democracy: Healing the Break Between People and Government* and editor of *Pathways Out of Poverty: Innovations in Microfinance for the Poorest Families,* about which Muhammad Yunus said, "If we are serious about the Millennium Development Goal of reducing poverty by half by 2015, we'll have no other option but to establish credit as a human right. This book will help guide you to do it."

Mr. Daley-Harris lives in Washington, DC, with his wife, Shannon, who is a consultant with the Religious Affairs Division of the Children's Defense Fund. Their son, Micah, was born in May 1998 and their daughter, Sophie, was born in May 2001.

Anna Awimbo

Anna Awimbo is Research Director of the Microcredit Summit Campaign. She has several years of experience working on women's and youth issues to help identify alternative strategies for poverty alleviation. Her work has included tracking data to monitor the Microcredit Summit Campaign's progress towards its goal. She co-designed and is part of the Summit's team that coordinates training in Africa and Asia on the systematic integration of microcredit with education in child survival, HIV/AIDS prevention, and reproductive health. Ms. Awimbo also serves on the

Business Advisory Council of Five Talents International, an Anglican initiative to combat poverty through microenterprise development.

Thierry van Bastelaer

Thierry van Bastelaer is a political economist and expert in social capital, collective action, and microenterprise. He is Director of Economic Opportunities at Save the Children/US where he works on strategy development of the organization's microenterprise programs. He was previously Director of the Enterprise Development Group at the University of Maryland's IRIS Center, which provides technical assistance and research targeted at the development of micro-, small, and medium enterprises in developing and transition economies. Dr. van Bastelaer managed a number of projects in this area, including the development of user-friendly poverty assessment tools for USAID microenterprise clients, an applied research program to identify the role of micro-enterprises in growth and poverty alleviation, and the development of toolkits for the reform of legal frameworks for microfinance and electronic commerce. His research also examined the impact of competition among microfinance providers in saturated markets.

Manfred Zeller

Manfred Zeller is a professor for Rural Development Theory and Policy at the University of Hohenheim, Germany. His research in Asia, Africa, and Latin America focuses on the analysis of food, agriculture, and rural development policies (including microfinance) and on the measurement of poverty. As a research fellow of the International Food Policy Research Institute (IFPRI), he led its multi-country program on rural financial policies and food security from 1993 to 1999.

Nigel Biggar

Nigel Biggar has over fourteen years of experience working with microenterprise and microfinance in developing countries. He began in this field working as a microentrepreneur with a street youth project he established in Quito, Ecuador, in the early 1990s. He has worked extensively with MFIs in Latin America and Asia.

He is currently the Manager of Social Performance at Grameen Foundation USA (GFUSA) and the principal for the Poverty Progress Index initiative. He previously served as GFUSA's Regional Director for the Americas, where he assisted start-up microcredit organizations in Latin

America in building and expanding their programs based on the Grameen methodology. He holds a master's degree in Development Studies from the Institute of Development Studies at Sussex University.

Rekha Reddy

Rekha Reddy is a Senior Director in the Research and Policy Division of ACCION International, where she is responsible for the measurement of poverty and social performance of ACCION affiliates and for the writing and editing of ACCION publications on microfinance.

Prior to joining ACCION in 2004, Ms. Reddy worked internationally at the microfinance organization Pro Mujer Mexico and at UNICEF Guatemala. She also served as a senior project manager at the New York City Economic Development Corporation and as an assistant economist in the International Research Division of the Federal Reserve Bank of New York. Ms. Reddy received her master's in Public Affairs (MPA) from the Woodrow Wilson School at Princeton University and a BA in economics from Columbia University.

Alex Counts

Alex Counts is President and CEO of Grameen Foundation (GF), a dynamic nonprofit, Washington, DC–based organization that has grown to a global network of fifty-two microfinance partners in twenty-two countries. Counts became GF's first Executive Director in 1997. A 1988 Cornell University graduate with a degree in economics, Counts has demonstrated a commitment to poverty eradication that deepened during his time as a Fulbright scholar witnessing dire poverty as well as innovative solutions in Bangladesh. He subsequently trained to be a catalyst for change under Dr. Muhammad Yunus, the founder and Managing Director of the Grameen Bank. He is the author of *Give Us Credit* (Random House, 1996), about Grameen Bank and its applications in inner-city settings in the United States.

Roshaneh Zafar

Roshaneh Zafar is the founder of the Kashf Foundation and a disciple of Muhammad Yunus, the founder of Grameen Bank. A graduate of Yale and Wharton, Ms. Zafar began her career at the World Bank, which she left in 1994 to work with poor women in her native Pakistan. In 1996, inspired by the Grameen Bank, Ms. Zafar founded the Kashf Foundation to provide small loans to poor women in Pakistan. Ms. Zafar was one of the first Ashoka Fellows in Pakistan and was recently selected as a Social Entrepreneur by the Schwab Foundation. In addition, she was awarded the Tamgha I Imtiaz, one of Pakistan's highest civilian awards, by the president of Pakistan in 2006 for her work in the field of development and women's empowerment. She is also on the board of several organizations, including MISFA Limited, Afghanistan, and is a member of the UN Advisors Group on inclusive financial services.

Erin Connor

Erin Connor grew up in Southeast Asia and graduated from the University of Michigan with a BA in Chinese Studies. Ms. Connor received her MA in International Development from American University, and she now works as Program Officer for Grameen Foundation's Post-Tsunami Microfinance Initiative.

Larry Reed

Larry Reed is the Chief Executive Officer of the Opportunity International Network, a global coalition of forty-two microfinance organizations in over twenty-five countries. Opportunity's member organizations include microfinance programs in Africa, Asia, Eastern Europe, and Latin America, and support offices in Australia, Canada, Germany, the United Kingdom, and the United States.

Beginning his service with Opportunity-US in 1984, Mr. Reed has held a variety of senior positions within the organization. In 1991 he founded Opportunity's Africa Regional Office in Zimbabwe, and he served as its Africa Regional Director until 1996. Upon returning to the United States, he became Vice President of Opportunity-US for global operations.

Opportunity internationalized its structure in 1998, and Mr. Reed was asked to lead the new Opportunity International Network.

From 1999 to 2002 he served as chair of the Small Education Enterprise Promotion (SEEP) network, a research and advocacy group of microfinance industry practitioners. He was also a plenary speaker at the 1999 Microcredit Summit Meeting of Councils in Abidjan, Ivory Coast, and a featured speaker on microfinance at the 1999 World Parliament of Religions Conference in Cape Town, South Africa. He also has published several articles on microfinance and served as a contributor to *The New World of Microfinance* (Rhyne, Otero, et al.,1996), *Serving with the Poor in Africa* (Yamamori, Myers, Bediako, and Reed, 1996) and *Globalization and the Kingdom of God* (Goudzwaard, 2001).

Mr. Reed is a graduate of Wheaton College and the John F. Kennedy School of Government at Harvard University. He and his wife, Sandy, live in Oak Park, Illinois, with their three teenage children.

Women's World Banking

Women's World Banking (WWB) is a global network of over fifty microfinance institutions and banks in over 40 countries in Asia, Africa, Latin America, Eastern Europe, and the Middle East. WWB's network members provide micro-lending services to over 18 million poor women and men, and savings services to millions more. Together, WWB network members aim to change the way the world works by connecting poor women to economic and financial systems locally and globally.

Poor women are at the center of what the WWB network does. The network reaches poor women by providing and organizing support to its member organizations, which in turn offer direct services to these women. In practical terms, this means creating the possibility for a low-income woman to build her business and assets, improve her living conditions, keep her family well fed and healthy, educate her children, develop respect at home and in her community, and secure a political voice.

WWB has been a leader in building a global consensus on performance standards for the microfinance industry, and in shaping policies and financial systems for the world's poor majority. By helping network members get what they need to succeed, and by helping shape financial systems and industry standards, WWB seeks to reduce the gap between the hundreds of millions of poor women who require financial services and those who currently receive micro-loans.

Also from Kumarian Press...

Global Development and Microfinance:

Globalization and Social Exclusion: A Transformationalist Perspective
Ronaldo Munck

Deeper than Debt: Economic Globalization and the Poor
George Ann Potter

Savings Services for the Poor
Edited by Madeline Hirschland

**The Commercialization of Microfinance: Balancing Business
and Development**
Edited by Deborah Drake and Elisabeth Rhyne, ACCION International

New and Forthcoming:

**A World Turned Upside Down: Social Ecological Approaches to Children
in War Zones**
Edited by Neil Boothby, Mike Wessells, and Alison Strang

Development and the Private Sector: Consuming Interests
Edited by Deborah Eade and John Sayer

**The Search for Empowerment: Social Capital as Idea and Practice
at the World Bank**
Edited by Anthony Bebbington, Michael Woolcock, Scott Guggenheim
and Elizabeth Olson

Transnational Civil Society: An Introduction
Edited by Srilatha Batliwala and L. David Brown

Visit Kumarian Press at www.kpbooks.com
or call toll-free 800.289.2664
for a complete catalog.

*Kumarian Press, located in Bloomfield, Connecticut, is a
forward-looking, scholarly press that promotes active international
engagement and an awareness of global connectedness.*